DATE DUE			

RIDING LONG DISTANCE

Riding Long Distance

Ann Hyland

J. A. Allen

London

British Library Cataloguing in Publication Data

Hyland, Ann
    Riding long distance. – (Allen's rider guides).
    1. ~~Livestock : Horses~~. Endurance riding ~~– Manuals~~ (*Horsemanship*)
    I. Title   *2. Horsemanship.*
    798.2'3

    ISBN 0–85131–470–8

Published in Great Britain by
J. A. Allen & Company Limited
1 Lower Grosvenor Place, Buckingham Palace Road,
London SW1W 0EL

Book production Bill Ireson

Printed in Great Britain by
WBC Print Ltd, Bristol

Contents

Illustrations

Tables

Preface

Over twenty years ago when I first got hooked on my special sport I blundered in the dark. I had a terrific horse and the desire to test her, plus the wonderful open trails for training where I lived in North Carolina, USA, but I did not have much deep knowledge. In fact I had so little specific knowledge of what I was tackling that I went into my first 100-mile ride thinking it was easy with such a good horse as my Magnet Regent. This is a mistake which tyros (newcomers to the sport) often make as they regard long distance riding as an extended trail ride or hack. We did well. I realized what a tremendous field of knowledge was opening up to me and, more important, I realized how much I did not know. The good endurance and long distance rider never knows enough, and he knows he does not. That stops him making costly and dangerous errors. I wish in those early years a publisher had had the foresight to offer newcomers a guide to the sport, and I hope the following chapters will assist those embarking on this compulsive activity.

Introduction

This book is intended to help encourage all riders who, while they already enjoy their horse's companionship riding out either singly or with a group of friends, wish to enlarge their scope and combine the pleasure of a ride with the spice of a competition.

In recent years the sport of long distance riding has become the fastest growing branch of equestrianism in Britain as well as in many other countries, not least the United States where the sport had its beginnings just over thirty years ago. This was when in the 1950s the now legendary Tevis Cup 100-Mile Endurance Ride was run for the first time. By the mid 1960s the sport had crossed the Atlantic and was taking root in that bastion of British equestrianism, the British Horse Society. Aided by the Arab Horse Society, the B.H.S. ran an increasingly popular series of qualifying rides culminating in the annual Golden Horseshoe event of first 50, then 75, and currently 100 miles run over two days. In the early 1970s the Endurance Horse and Pony Society of Great Britain (E.H.P.S.) was formed and it embarked on a very ambitious programme of both Competitive Trail Rides (C.T.R.) and Endurance Rides (E.R.). They ran the first 100-mile in one day Endurance Ride in England. Scotland was feeling the lack of ride venues, all counties of England and Wales being well catered for by one or both societies, and in self-defence started the Highland Long Distance Riding Club in 1983. This is now expanding rapidly with a network of rides over Scotland.

The events held by these associations offer something for every level of equine and human competence on the long distance trail, and the following chapters examine aspects of this rapidly growing sport, from the inviting low distance pleasure rides to the threshold of competition and on to the challenge of the longer, tougher, faster rides.

The number of people in Britain who ride is growing rapidly, and though many are restricted to attending riding schools, hacking or trekking stables, horse ownership now extends to a large proportion of riders. Many do not wish to enter the specialized fields of showing, jumping, eventing, or dressage, or cannot do so because of the prohibitive cost. On the long distance trail one meets a greater variety of horses than in any other equestrian sport, including the custom-built Arabian so well designed for endurance riding, the hunter, the cob, almost all of the British native breeds, the well-loved British partbreds, and a proportion of imported breeds, amongst them the Trakehner, Quarter Horse, Morgan and Andalusian. There is hardly a breed that is not successful in a ride somewhere in a season's events. And the major bonus? Success is not measured by the few top placings. Every horse who passes the final veterinary examination is a winner! The system itself is designed to encourage the rider to aim higher with his or her special horse.

1 Definitions

Long distance riding encompasses several categories of events.

Pleasure Rides

These are rides where there is no competitive element. Distances are usually between 15 and 25 miles. Horses must be a minimum of four years of age to enter, and in events run by the recognized distance riding societies this will be stated in the ride schedule. There is usually a minimum speed, imposed mainly to make sure stewards are not kept on course for an excessive length of time, and to assist organizers in tracking entries. Should any horse be long overdue then it is a warning that the rider may be lost, or that something untoward has happened, and the people at ride base are then alerted. There are usually very attractive rosettes awarded to all horses who complete the distance.

Training Rides

These are run to acquaint newcomers to the sport with the feel of riding in a competition without the real competitive element. They will be of a similar distance to a pleasure ride, but will have a minimum speed imposed nearer that required in actual competition, and the event will be under simulated competitive ride rules.

Competitive Events

The two main categories of competitive rides are Competitive Trail Rides (C.T.R.) and Endurance Rides (E.R.). They are run by the main associations and although the associations' rules may vary slightly the broad scope of each division is very similar. Within the scope of Competitive Trail and Endurance Rides there are many different events which will be dealt with in Chapter 3.

COMPETITIVE TRAIL RIDES These rides are judged on a 'speed and condition' basis. Competing horses must complete the course at a required minimum speed and pass the veterinary examination at the finish of the ride. Points will be deducted should the horse's final condition warrant it. According to the veterinary score the horse will be awarded a completion award, and in most rides a grading award as well. Distances start at 20 miles and range through to 60 miles in one day.

ENDURANCE RIDES These are rides run against the clock and the fastest horse is the winner. However, he and all other competing horses must pass the final veterinary examination and, in the veterinary surgeon's opinion, be capable of continuing further should it be deemed necessary. In other words he may not finish in an exhausted or bad clinical state and still receive a completion award. Distances start at 40 miles and range through to 100 miles in a day. Some Endurance Rides may be split into a two-day ride but still have the speed element deciding the winner.

RIDE AND TIE This event is for teams of three – one horse and two riders. The two riders take turns in running and riding, tying the horse at designated stations en route. The rider dismounts, ties the horse, and proceeds to the next station on foot, while the runner behind catches up, unties the horse and rides to the next station, overtaking the runner; and so on to the finish. The winning team is the first to have all three across the line. The horse must pass the final veterinary check to qualify for an award.

THE ARAB HORSE SOCIETY MARATHON This comes under the category of endurance riding, though it is of shorter duration than the rides run by the other associations, being comparable to the human marathon event. It is open to horses of any breed, even though run by the Arab Horse Society.

2 The Associations

In England we have two major associations and in Scotland one, all of which cater to the long distance riding enthusiast. All offer a series of rides that give the rider new to the sport a chance to progress from easy to moderate, difficult, and then extremely challenging rides. Young and novice horses have plenty of events which test their ability without overstressing them. In addition to the major associations many riding clubs offer the occasional pleasure or competitive ride for members and their friends.

The British Horse Society Long Distance Riding Group

The B.H.S. L.D.R.G. is one of the four disciplines of the British Horse Society. To participate in most of their rides it is necessary to be a member of both the parent association and the L.D.R.G. In addition the horse must also be entered in the Long Distance Riding Registry on an annual basis. Membership is open to riders ten years of age and over. Registered horses must be a minimum of five years of age, with the exception of the Bronze Buckle Series where four-year-old horses may compete. The L.D.R.G. is based at B.H.S. Headquarters and prospective members should write to The Secretary, The British Horse Society Long Distance Riding Group, British Equestrian Centre, Stoneleigh, Kenilworth, Warwickshire, CV8 2LR. All members receive a very comprehensive rule book and annual schedule of rides together with the official entry forms.

The Endurance Horse and Pony Society of Great Britain

This association offers all types of long distance ride. It is not necessary to be a member to take part in E.H.P.S. rides. However, non-members pay a considerably higher entrance fee for each ride. The horses do not need to be registered with the society before they compete. Riders eight years and over are eligible to compete, but riders under ten years of age are only allowed to ride a maximum of 30 miles.

Horses must be a minimum of four years of age, but they may only be ridden in pleasure rides and/or novice Competitive Trail Rides, and may not accrue any trophy points or be awarded gradings until they are five years old. All members receive a Competitors' Reference Book, but make separate application for entry forms for each ride. The E.H.P.S. has many area groups that organize their own schedule of rides under E.H.P.S. rules, in addition to the main society's schedule of events. The E.H.P.S. of G.B. Membership Secretary, to whom all applications for membership should be sent, is Ossie Hare, Mill House, Mill Lane, Stoke Bruerne, Northants, NN12 7SH.

The Highland Long Distance Riding Club

The club offers a diverse range of rides from pleasure events to competitive rides run by the Area Branches with distances of up to 40 miles. In addition to other classes, the Central Club organizes the annual Scottish Championships, involving the Open Championship of 75 miles and the Novice Championship which follows a 25-mile course. Though founded considerably later than the other associations the H.L.D.R.C. is spreading rapidly, with new branches constantly being added to the nucleus of Argyll, Glasgow, Inverness, Tayside, and Angus. Because of the nature of much of Scotland's terrain I am informed by Candy Cameron (who supplied me with H.L.D.R.C. details) that the 'miles seem a lot longer than English ones'! Rules are similar to those used by the B.H.S. L.D.R.G. Encouragement is given to all riders in the form of awards for cumulative mileage, starting with 100 miles, then 250 and thereafter in increments of 250 miles. Lectures and clinics on subjects related to long distance riding are held during the winter months. The address to contact for Scottish readers interested in competing is Ellan Ann Stephens, The Highland Long Distance Riding Club, Rowanlea, North Kessock, By Inverness, Scotland.

Periodic Literature

All three societies publish a newsletter or bulletin with relevant endurance riding news several times a year. Many equestrian magazines give the sport coverage, reporting events and offering useful articles. *Horse and Hound* gives major ride results, and the bi-monthly magazine *Distance Rider* reports on all aspects of British and European distance riding, including the latest technical advances being made in the sport. A comprehensive survey of long distance riding is Ann Hyland's, *The Endurance Horse* (J. A. Allen, 1988), which describes the sport in great detail and contains sections on all the countries currently involved.

3 The Stepping Stones

The major societies offer a graded system of rides to ease horses and riders new to long distance riding into the sport. Their rules offer stringent safeguards for the horses. With the exception of pleasure rides all events are run under very tight veterinary supervision, and the veterinary judges' decisions are final. No horse may proceed if either at the beginning of or during a ride the veterinary surgeon considers it in the animal's best interests to withdraw him. Throughout the ride there is constant veterinary monitoring so that any animal suffering undue stress is eliminated. To earn an end-of-ride award the horse must be in a good clinical condition and capable of proceeding further. This is a technicality, but in practice means that the horse must have plenty of reserve left at the finish. He must not be in an exhausted state, or have received an injury such as a bad laceration to the limb, a severe abrasion of the mouth, or a saddle or girth gall likely to render it painful for him to proceed. At one time, when C.T.R.s offered individual placings plus completion awards, any horses tying on points did have to proceed for a further distance to determine exact placings, or a veterinary surgeon who was judging could call on a further distance to be ridden. Now the rule simply means that the horse must be *capable* of going a further distance.

The stepping stones that a horse uses in his progression from being a Novice C.T.R. horse to an Open C.T.R. horse and then into the E.R. category are designed to offer an increasing challenge while not overburdening a young horse. Young and/or inexperienced horses start in shorter distanced rides run at moderate speeds. Before going into the next strata of competition, where the speed will be one or two miles an hour faster, and the

18

distance considerably longer, they need to qualify by achieving a certain standard. Once they have achieved this standard in the middle category they are permitted to upgrade to the higher echelons of the sport.

The best way of illustrating this, and to avoid confusion for a newcomer to the sport, is to give examples of one horse competing in the B.H.S. L.D.R.G., and another horse competing in the E.H.P.S. series of rides. Although these two groups offer what at first glance may seem a confusing array of rides, study of their complete rules issued upon gaining membership will show the prospective competitor that the main aim is the same – to take a horse safely through several seasons of competition – and that the differences are mainly a matter of nomenclature. Both groups acknowledge the good done by the other and have a reciprocal system whereby to qualify for some of their major rides each accepts the qualifications gained in rides run by the other society.

Two Careers

In illustrating the careers of two horses I am taking the baseline of both horses being four years of age, which is the youngest they may enter rides. The schedule of events for both societies is so structured that any rider who wishes to compete in long distance riding will find something within his/her capabilities and suitable for horses of all breeds and sizes. First-time long distance riders will be encouraged by events which though testing them and their horses are not so demanding as to leave them wondering whatever made them enter. Indeed, new competitors usually find the ride not nearly as difficult as anticipated, and coupled with the feeling of achievement the wish to go on to longer rides is usually lurking in the background and takes only a few more rides to turn into a definite urge.

Both societies have long competitive seasons, and the Highland Long Distance Riding Club season, with rides similar to those run by the B.H.S. L.D.R.G., extends in the main from February to October with some rides being held outside this span in the areas with a milder climate. B.H.S. L.D.R.G. competitive rides start in mid-February, and the E.H.P.S. opts for a slightly later start in March. There are occasional pleasure and training rides run even earlier. The longer mileage events tend to come later in the season, thus giving horses and riders a chance to ease gradually into each seasons's competitions. This aspect is most welcome as the mid-winter training schedule is governed by the lack of long light evenings. For many riders, especially those with a Monday-to-Friday nine-to-five job, lengthy training rides have to be done at weekends.

B.H.S. L.D.R.G. RIDES The B.H.S. L.D.R.G. schedule of events offers the four-year-old horse a series of rides in the Bronze Buckle category. These consist of Qualifying Rides of 20 miles which are run at a minimum average speed of 6.5 m.p.h., and Bronze Buckle Final rides of 30 miles, run at a minimum average speed of 7 m.p.h. These rides give young horses experience of long distance riding plus introducing them to the activity connected with any competitive event, such as unfamiliar surroundings in which there seems to be an awful lot going on for a horse in his first away-from-home events. There are plenty of Bronze Buckle Qualifiers scattered through the season, and from April onwards there are Final rides held in conjunction with other Official Rides. A rider may upgrade his/her horse at the pace and level of experience suited to that horse, and not be restricted to a single chance to enter a final event in each season, though once through a final they must upgrade. For the Bronze Buckle Qualifiers membership in the L.D.R.G. and registration of the horse in the B.H.S. L.D.R.G. Registry is not required. However, riders wishing to enter the Bronze Buckle Final must be fully paid-up members. This offers new long distance riders ample opportunity to decide if they wish to be more deeply involved in the sport before they incur the additional expenditure of membership and registration fees.

The next stage is the Silver Stirrup Series of rides. Horses must be a minimum of five years of age to compete and the Qualifying Rides are run over a 40-mile course at a minimum average speed of 7 m.p.h. while the final is run over a 50-mile course at 7½ m.p.h. After a horse has successfully negotiated Bronze Buckle and Silver Stirrup stages he will have had at least two seasons of gradually increasing distance and speed behind him if he started as a four-year-old. If he started as a five-year-old it is possible to upgrade in both divisions within one season, but not advisable for such a young horse. If the horse is much older and therefore physically mature and already used to regular work it would be in order to take the two stages in one year, provided they were spaced over the entire season. He can go no further than Silver Stirrup stage as a five-year-old but must wait till he is six before embarking on the Gold Series of rides, which are 75 miles or more in length and usually run over several days, with the exception of a limited number of 100-mile in one day rides.

For all B.H.S. L.D.R.G. rides it is the rider who qualifies, not the horse, *with the exception* of the Golden Horseshoe Final, for which both horse and rider must qualify annually. Under this system it takes three years to take a horse through the full range of events offered by the B.H.S. L.D.R.G.

E.H.P.S. OF G.B. RIDES   A similar system operates with this society. The four-year-old may enter pleasure rides and the Novice series of rides which have a minimum distance of 20 and a maximum length of 25 miles. However, in competitive rides he may only receive a completion award and may not earn any points towards any of the annual trophies. Novice rides are run at a minimum average speed of 6 m.p.h., and the horse may not exceed an average of 7 m.p.h. Times outside this bracket incur time penalties.

As a five-year-old he may enter Novice Competitive Trail Rides, be awarded points on a time and condition basis and be graded according to his score, and he may earn points towards the annual national awards. Five-year-old horses may also enter the full range of C.T.R. events, in which there is a large selection of distances and speeds and two categories. The Open Rides range from 25 to a maximum of 60 miles in one day and speeds are between 7 and 8 m.p.h. for a perfect time score with time penalties between 5–7 and 8–9 m.p.h. Speeds outside this range incur disqualification. The other C.T.R. category is Fast C.T.R. events where the distances range between 25 and 35 miles and speeds 8 to 9 m.p.h. for a perfect time score, with penalties between 6–8 and 9–10 m.p.h. and disqualification outside these limits.

As a six-year-old the horse may enter the Endurance Ride section, but must first qualify by achieving a grade in two 40-mile or over C.T.R.s, or a grade in one C.T.R. run by the E.H.P.S. and an award in one B.H.S. Golden Horseshoe Qualifier or Golden

Horseshoe Final. In the E.H.P.S. both horse and rider must qualify to enter an Endurance Ride.

To compete in the E.H.P.S. Summer Solstice 100-Mile One-Day Ride, horses must be a minimum of seven years of age and the rider and horse must have completed at least one 50-mile Endurance Ride with the E.H.P.S. or finished a Golden Horseshoe Final at a minimum speed of 7 m.p.h. This must have been achieved within the previous twelve months. The only exception to this rule is that a horse that has completed the 100-mile ride in any previous year does not have to requalify, though of course it is in the horse's interests to make sure he has had enough build-up in competition preparation before each attempt at the 100 miler.

From this broad outline readers can see that promising young horses are safeguarded by restricting their participation to a level suitable to their maturity and degree of ability. All young horses take time to mature and their competitive life will be prolonged by many years if they are introduced to the sport gradually, their events being well spaced and their riders using them judiciously, not burning them out in one or two seasons. The real successes of an endurance horse are measured not only by wins and places, but by the number of years he competes and comes through season after season sound in wind, limb and mind.

If a rider new to long distance riding is entering an older horse for his first ride and is, therefore, according to the rules of the E.H.P.S. permitted to enter Open C.T.R. rides of the longest category without going through the Novice strata, he/she would be well advised not to tackle the maximum permitted. He/she should take things slowly and start with at least three or four of the shorter distanced rides in order to learn the ropes before tackling any more ambitious event. The B.H.S. L.D.R.G. structure imposes its own restraint by requiring new horses and riders to start with the Bronze before upgrading to the Silver strata.

Long distance riding, provided it is tackled sensibly, rapidly changes from the occasional event to a way of life, with the competitions being the highspots. Riders will find themselves planning a series of rides, then a season, and ultimately a career for one or more horses.

Lifetime Qualifications

Once a horse and rider have achieved a completion in either an E.H.P.S. 100 miler or a B.H.S. L.D.R.G. Golden Horseshoe Final, the rider carries that qualification thereafter. However, the horse must still go through the qualification system. In effect this means that should a qualified rider be offered a ride on a horse qualified by another rider he/she can take up the option of a ride in the E.H.P.S. 100 miler, or go straight into B.H.S. Gold rides. Occasionally a rider does have two horses qualified and will welcome an experienced rider who for one or another reason does not have his/her own horse to ride.

Riders are not restricted to competing with one society but, if paid-up members, may avail themselves of an even wider range of events throughout each season. Care should be taken not to overburden any horse with an excessive number of rides.

4 Horses for Courses

Most riders entering a long distance ride for the first time do so because they are curious to find out more about it; see if their horse is capable of succeeding in a new equine sport; or because a friend enjoys it and has persuaded them to 'have a go'. Consequently they nearly always begin their long distance involvement with the horse they are currently riding.

It is only when riders opt for total committment and plan a full season of competitions with the eventual aim of entering the longer, tougher rides that selection of a specific horse becomes necessary.

The Suitability of the Horse

For the lower distances and slower speeds any fit, sound horse should be quite capable of achieving successful completion awards and with the easier rides a quite high grade as well. Grades are assessed on the time taken and the number of veterinary penalties deducted.

When using the horse you are currently riding assess his good points, and even more important be very aware of his faults.

MAIN ASSETS The horse should have a generally good conformation allied with a generous but easy-going disposition so that he gives of his best willingly but is not over eager. Willingness means the rider tires less quickly and the easy-going disposition will help the horse conserve energy.

HEAD AND NECK The head should be refined with a large, alert eye. The jawbones should be spaced far enough apart to allow ample room for the windpipe. The neck should be moderately long and meet the head at an angle that permits excellent wind passage. Too heavy a head often indicates that a horse will travel on his forehand, and a constriction in the gullet where the head joins the neck would impair free passage of air.

THE WITHERS   These should be capable of holding a saddle well, without the need to use either a breastplate, except in very hilly going, or a crupper.

THE BACK   The back should be moderately short with a very strong loin area.

THE BARREL AND RIB-CAGE   The rib-cage should be well sprung, giving sufficient breadth to the barrel without being so broad that the rider's legs are uncomfortably spread. Too narrow a spread does not allow sufficient room for internal organs to perform to maximum capacity. A too narrow, weedy horse rarely succeeds at top level.

THE CHEST   This should be reasonably broad allowing plenty of room for heart and lungs. Too broad a chest often gives a jarring, stilted ride, while a narrow, pinched-in chest does not allow sufficient room for internal organs.

THE SHOULDERS   The shoulders should slope, ideally, at a 45 degree angle and this should be followed through with the same angle of slope in pastern and hoof.

THE QUARTERS   These should be powerful without being massive. They should have a well-pronounced inner thigh muscle. Frequently horses lacking this tend to brush.

THE LEGS   The legs should be clean, tendons well delineated, joints sufficiently large, with no puffy swellings (curbs, thorough-pins, spavins, etc.).

THE HOOVES   They should be hard but the horn should also be resilient and not liable to cracking or splitting. The soles should be concave to prevent susceptibility to stonebruising. The frog should be well defined and able to carry out its natural function of absorbing shock. As with other parts of the horse the dimensions should be moderate, neither too small a hoof for the weight it has to bear nor the overlarge, flat 'dinner plate' variety that frequently is heir to other undesirable characteristics such as soft horn or dropped sole.

THE OVERALL LOOK   The horse should present a picture where each part melds well. Too light a frame and the horse may not be up to the eventual severity of tougher rides. Too heavy a build and the horse will give a ride tiring both to himself and his rider. The ideal is a horse of good proportions with a medium but strong build.

Condition

It is very important not to confuse a light-framed horse with a horse that is in very lean and fit condition. It is vital that the horse's condition is monitored throughout training. It is dangerous to campaign a horse in gross condition. Such a horse puts undue strain on his limbs, his heart and his lungs. However, I have noted and with concern that the opposite condition of

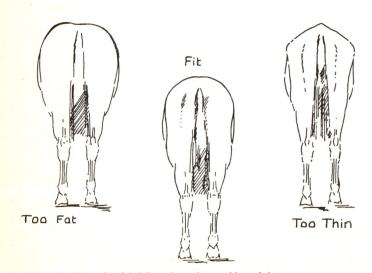

Condition: (*left*) too fat, (*right*) too lean, (*centre*) just right.

26

excessive thinness is more prevalent now that long distance riding is becoming increasingly popular. Some inexperienced riders are confusing thinness with the horse being lean and fit, and there are some horses being ridden that show the poverty line in the hindquarters. These horses often have rather dry lack-lustre coats without that essential layer of reserve condition covering their frames. It does take an exceedingly watchful eye and good management to determine and maintain the horse in ideal condition over a full season. Be alert. Be critical. And be prepared to ask advice if necessary.

Choosing a Horse

If, after competing in a few rides, a rider feels it is imperative to purchase a horse specifically for long distance riding, take plenty of time making the choice. Study results of as many rides as possible. Get back-numbers of newsletters and bulletins from the long distance riding societies and analyse which horses are most consistent. This does not mean only the horses that win the big rides, but the horses that consistently gain completions in the tougher rides. These horses may also get high gradings or out-right wins as well, but it is the frequency with which their names appear in the completions lists that will be the guide to their ability over one or more seasons. Analysis of specific breed performance levels will become obvious, and you will be able to make a reasoned choice of your future mount.

Having said that, it has become apparent over the years that certain breeds are superior to others, particularly when the chips are down in the top echelons of Endurance Riding, but it is still best to do a little research on your own, as well as being helped towards your future choice by advice from seasoned distance riders. Trusting blindly to promotional advice from breed societies is not the best way to be influenced towards future purchase. Almost all breed societies will claim identical attributes for their own breed, such as superb temperament; generosity; soundness; versatility; suitability as a first-class trail horse, and so on.

In spite of the above statement, which is intended mainly as a warning to do your own research as well as advising you to obtain help, it is clear that there are several breeds that excel on the long distance, C.T.R., and more specifically the Endurance trail. Number one in almost every country, and especially in the three major endurance riding countries of America, Australia and Great Britain, is the Arabian and his related kin. Study of results from Great Britain alone will show that horses of Arabian blood have excelled right from the start, and a brief catalogue from the E.H.P.S. of G.B. results will suffice to show what I mean.

The E.H.P.S. archives show results right from the start of their competitive rides and the top places in their four major annual trophies show a marked consistency by horses of Arabian breeding. The results shown below are taken from the first fourteen years of the records, although some trophies were not offered right from the beginning. But starting with the Open Championship, which was the first major trophy awarded, pure or partbred Arabians have placed as follows:

The Open Championship – 7 wins and 4 reserves in fourteen years
The Novice Championship – 9 wins and 8 reserves in twelve years
The Competitive Trail Trophy – 7 wins in twelve years
The Endurance Trophy – 7 wins in eleven years.

When Great Britain sends a team abroad the majority of members have, to date, been mounted on horses of Arabian breeding. The first World Champion, Cassandra Schuler, and runner up, Jeannie Waldron, both rode purebred Arabians. The triple winner of Australia's premier Endurance Ride, the Tom Quilty 100 Miler, is Glenallon Solomon, a partbred Arabian. Indeed, the two equines with the most miles under their girths in Australia are both part Arabian: Juanita, a partbred Arabian mule, has nearly 8,000 km to her credit, and Andarra Shareef, an Anglo-Arabian, is hot on her heels. The best-known American ride is the Tevis Cup, the prototype for all other 100 mile in one day rides, and out of thirty-two Tevis Cups thirty have been won by horses of Arabian blood – one purebred, Witezarif, having won it six times! In ten starts our own Summer Solstice 100 miler has been won four times by purebreds, once by an Anglo-Arabian, and twice by partbreds.

Britain has a preponderence of partbreds of many breeds. Arabian and Thoroughbred blood is most often infused with one of the many native pony breeds. Those stemming from the larger of the native breeds such as New Forest, Connemara and Welsh Cob have done very well in long distance riding. There are also many breeds relatively new to Great Britain and amongst the ranks of successful breeds represented are Morgan, Appaloosa, Quarter Horse, Trakehner and Haflinger. Some are purebred and others crossed with indigenous breeds, amongst which for this chapter's purpose I include the Arabian and the Thoroughbred.

INHERITED AND ACQUIRED CHARACTERISTICS When purchasing a horse for long distance riding if at all possible research into the horse's parents. Were they proven in stressful performance? What were their temperaments? What was their soundness record? In particular, were they prone to any leg ailments or wind disorders – two of the vital aspects in long distance riding? If retired from competition were they retired sound, or because of injury, which is acceptable, or because of a breakdown, which is not acceptable?

I recommend avoiding purchase of any horse that has been subjected to strenuous work too early in life. This does not mean that no horse that has been subjected to stress as a youngster will be successful, but I would not want a query in that department. I would not buy an ex-racehorse if another candidate with all the other assets listed in this chapter was available. Nor would I buy a horse that had been excessively showjumped at an early age. In both cases too much strain has been put on the limbs and joints.

VETERINARY EXAMINATION Before concluding purchase get a very detailed veterinary examination of the horse. I recommend going to the extra expense of x-raying the lower limb. This is where most trouble arises in the long distance horse.

COST If you intend entering the really tough rides after your 'apprenticeship' in the lower mileage classes, do not economize on the initial purchase. For too long purchasers looking for a prospective endurance horse had a blind spot when it came to paying a reasonable price for him. The old idea that it did not require any particular talent for this sport was prevalent. A horse you intend taking to the top does require talent, so an economy made at purchase time could be extremely costly in later disappointment and lack of future success, not to mention the wasted time and money for zero results. The sport has expanded to such an extent, particularly in Britain, that a top endurance horse is a real specialist nowadays, and is ranked in the esteem of many who appreciate his performance with that of top eventers and showjumpers.

5 Basic Care of the Long Distance Horse

Everyday Care

To get the best out of the horse it is essential that he is well maintained. Most riders have a full-time job so the care of the horse must fit around their working hours, especially on week-days, but do try to keep to a sensible pattern. The real key to keeping any horse, including the long distance horse, is moderation.

FEED Feed at regular times, but do not be absolutely tied to the clock. That induces undesirable habits with the horse demanding his rations, frequently in a bad-tempered way. Use the best quality feedstuffs available. These are not necessarily the most expensive. Study the analysis of proprietary brands. If your horse is only doing the short to moderate distance rides it is not necessary to have him on the rations prescribed for horses at the highest levels of performance. I am not going into a discourse on the various brand feeds as there are so many of them available, with new ones constantly being offered. However, the harder the horse works the more grain will be needed in his diet and the higher the protein requirements. A high performance level means the horse burns a lot of fuel, and feeds high in carbohydrates will be needed to replace energy, proteins to maintain the tissues at efficiency level, and minerals to sustain the body's correct metabolic balance. Your veterinary surgeon's advice is the best on the subject, not necessarily your feed merchant's.

The main constituents I like to see in a good diet for a horse in hard work are barley (crushed) and oats (crimped or crushed), some maize, and salt – either added regularly to the feed or if the horse will utilize it a permanent mineral salt lick in his stable (some will not touch it, so judicious addition of salt to the feed will have to be made). I also like to feed a proportion, usually about 4 lb per day, of alfalfa (lucerne) cubes to the horse's diet. They are high in protein and have a very good and consistent feed value. They are particularly good if top quality hay is hard to come by. One disadvantage to these cubes is that during summer when fresh grass is available my own distance horses will not touch them. An ex-distance horse, retired through *anno domini*, who is a very greedy individual eats them with relish even though he is getting good grass. You will have to see what your own horse will consume.

A basic guide to quantities of feed geared to the work a horse is doing is given in the table. It is only a guide, though, and in the hay department the amount shown is a minimum to be offered and assuming the horse has no access to grazing. I prefer to feed the horse all the hay he wants, with the exception of the compulsive eater who gorges. With that type of 'Billy Bunter' I restrict the hay ration.

Suggested rations per 100 lb bodyweight

Daily work	Grain	Hay
Maintenance or light work up to one hour daily	0·50 lb	1·50 lb
Two hours average work at steady rate	0·80 lb	1·50 lb
Three to four hours steady or two hours hard work	1·00 lb	1·50 lb
Medium hard work up to six hours steady or three hours hard work	1·25 lb	1·25 lb
Later stages of training for very tough rides	1·50 lb	1·25 lb

Newcomers to long distance riding who elect to take things slowly will be taking their horses up to the middle of the table in regard to work level. Apart from the day off when rations should be cut back the amount per day should be steady, as on very hard days with the horse maybe a little tired he will have expended more energy than his food replaces and will 'borrow' the deficit from days where energy expended was not as great as the fuel intake.

STABLING Our climate dictates that most horses are stabled all or part of the year. Inclement weather, particularly wet weather, will pull condition off a horse faster than hard work if he has to survive out of doors in the winter. He *must have access* to a dry haven, either a proper stable, or a well-bedded field shelter that has at least part of its front closed so he can get away from bitter winds and rain. It is not sufficient to place the shelter away from the prevailing wind as wind comes from all quarters at some time or other. If a horse has to be kept out, put well-tamped-down hardcore around the entrance to the field shelter as the poached muddy conditions will induce heel problems such as cracks, mud fever, or soreness. If possible also make sure that the shelter is on slightly raised ground so moisture drains away from, not into, the shelter floor.

If a horse is stabled most of the time, in addition to his regular exercise he should also have access to a paddock, or lacking that even a small turn-out area. Many leg problems can be ameliorated or prevented if the horse is allowed to unwind naturally by gentle movement. It also does wonders for his mind, helping to settle him and give him a more enjoyable existence. Again the keynote is moderation – enough freedom to keep him happy, and enough exercise for fitness, but the comfort of a loosebox or shelter against cold, wet and wind, and in summer heat and flies. Be generous with bedding. It is more economical in the long run, and will encourage the horse to rest properly.

Periodic Care

THE HOOVES The farrier should attend to the horse's feet on a regular basis. Shoes need replacing or resetting (according to state of wear) at approximately monthly intervals. The longest they should be left is six weeks. Owners will find a long distance horse goes through considerably more sets of shoes than horses in other fields of endeavour, and a re-set is rarely possible. All ride rules require the horse's shoes to be in good condition, so the normal practice is to shoe a few days before a ride. This gives time, should anything be wrong, to get it corrected. Risen clenches can cause nasty cuts, particularly on a tiring horse which will tend to interfere more than a horse that is fresh. Worn shoes predispose the horse to slipping and a bad slip could cause a torn muscle and subsequent lameness. Shoeing with heavier shoes because of the extra work is *inadvisable*. It will result in a heavier way of going and will not extend the shoe life. Calkins and studs are not recommended as they alter the angle of hoof placement.

TEETH   It is advisable, particularly with an older horse, to have his teeth checked at least annually. If he is passing any appreciable amount of grain in his droppings it is necessary, as he will not be getting the maximum benefit from his food. Also, should he start to chew on one side only, or drop food out of his mouth (with the exception of the habitually messy feeder), have his teeth checked.

WORMING   This should be done on a regular basis. Every two months is best. Vary the type of medicine used so the worms (of which there is always a residue left, usually in the larval or egg stage, even with the best medicines) do not get a tolerance to any one type of anthelmintic. At least once a year worm for bots. These have an annual cycle. The eggs are laid by the bot fly on the horse's front legs, shoulders, and portion of the mane near the withers during the latter part of the summer. This fly looks like a bee and hovers around these parts. It does not alight but shoots its eggs out. The horse then ingests the eggs which migrate in larval stage from the mouth to the stomach, where they have a happy time eating away while attached to the stomach lining. In spring they are passed in the dung in a chrysalis that looks like a red beetle. They hatch and the cycle starts again. It is no good worming for bots until the horse has completely shed his summer coat which carries the eggs. Mid-winter, when the bot has passed to the digestive tract, is the best time. Picking the droppings up daily from the paddock helps reduce the worm burden, but however clean you keep the paddock there will be some degree of re-infestation with parasites.

VACCINATIONS   Some of the major rides are now run from racecourses and all racecourse authorities require horses to have an up-to-date series of injections against equine influenza. Many horses have been turned away from ride venues because vaccinations were not in order, so do check with your own veterinary surgeon that your horse's vaccinations are according to Jockey Club Rules. It is worthwhile planning the series of injections so that the annual booster comes at a time when the horse is normally resting or in very light work, then the week of rest after the injection advised by most veterinary surgeons will not interrupt the horse's training schedule.

CLIPPING If your horse has an excessively heavy coat it is advisable to clip him either prior to starting work in the winter or, at the latest, before he embarks on the harder stages of his training. Some horses are fortunate in growing a very light coat and these can be left unclipped. Blanketing will help reduce coat growth, but as the long distance horse's annual lay-off period usually coincides with early and mid-winter months when he should be turned out daily there will be a battle to keep the mud off his coat. I do not like New Zealand rugs. I do not use them, and those I have seen used rarely seem to fit the horse properly, being in varying stages of disarray and uselessness. When they are not in place they chafe where most pressure is incorrectly placed. When clipping in winter leave the leg hair on, and do not trim the fetlocks, unless it is a carty type of horse, and even then leave enough feather on to protect the heels of the horse. Some horses, particularly those entering the very long, fast rides, benefit from clipping even in summer if they have thicker than average coats.

6 Schooling

Not so very long ago when long distance and endurance riding were in their formative years little attention was paid to schooling the competitive horse. The sport was new; few people in Great Britain had much experience, although a handful had acquired some experience in other countries. There was no instructional literature available to the newcomer, and it took many years for the endurance horse to be accorded the esteem he now enjoys. It was often felt that if a horse did not fit into one of the established competitive fields he could always do endurance riding, as that activity did not require any specific attributes or training. No prizes would be awarded at the end of the competition for the manner in which the horse accomplished the ride mileage!

At first many events were notable for the lack of horsemanship amongst riders. Many possible completions were thrown away in the early stages of a ride because the riders did not know how to get the best from their horses, and in the main allowed the horse to burn himself out too early in the ride either because he was undisciplined and allowed to rid himself of excessive energy before settling down, or the riders themselves considered the ride had to be one mad gallop from start to finish.

Costly errors have brought circumspection and a more enlightened way of tackling ride routes. In my opinion it is essential that the long distance and endurance horse receives a very sound basic training before he even starts on his actual long distance riding career.

This is not a manual on basic schooling but a few points need to be made about specific areas of training, and in the following sections reasons are given for ensuring that certain aspects are included in the general instruction the young horse receives.

Basic Training

In preliminary training the young horse is taught to respond to the aids and to carry himself with ease, and to employ strong, forward–moving paces. He should move in a balanced manner with all his propulsion coming from the hindquarters. Far too many horses are very heavily on the forehand and this way of going puts undue strain on the forelimbs. It is most noticeable that by far the highest percentage of lamenesses, which automatically result in elimination from rides, occur in the front legs. Many such lamenesses could be avoided if the horses were better schooled and used themselves more efficiently.

The way a long distance horse travels differs from the manner in which an ordinary pleasure horse works. Most riders keep the horse constantly on the bit, or rather they think they are keeping

Moving forward freely without rein restraint. The rider shows an independent seat.

the horse on the bit, or on contact. Frequently the horse is *in contact* with the bit, but not *on contact* in the accepted manner, merely leaning on the bit and the rider's hands for support. This predisposes the horse to travelling on the forehand and leads to a vicious circle. Should the rider relax the reins the horse loses his support and becomes clumsy and quite often stumbles. The rider may also feel insecure as the horse was being used as a prop by that rider just as much as he too was being supported by that rider – a 'no win' situation. The horse must learn to travel forward very freely without constant rein restraint. In his turn the rider must acquire an independent seat, not relying on the reins for his own support. There are occasions when a rider may need to help a horse down very steep inclines, or over other hazardous going, by a certain amount of rein restraint. If the horse has a constant rein constriction he will be unaware of such help and, being on the forehand, liable to make costly and dangerous mistakes. On the other hand once the rein restraint is relaxed the horse should not take it as permission to tank off. The office to increase speed comes from leg aids, and/or by shifting the rider's weight forward, and the well-schooled horse should wait until so asked.

OBEDIENCE   The horse must be taught instant obedience to the rider's wishes. By that I mean he must obey the aids to move on as soon as they are given. He must also slow down or stop when asked. It is not sufficient to decrease his speed by the normal drawn-out process whereby the rider pulls the reins until the horse more or less decreases his speed. This is accepted by far too many riders in all equestrian fields. The horse moving in this manner is usually boring on the bit, unpleasant to ride, and a danger to himself on the distance trail where hazards arise that do not present themselves in the course of everyday riding, such as precipitous climbs or loose footing. His mouth also takes a toll, becoming more or less insensitive. If the battle over speed is prolonged frequent bruising or even laceration of the mouth could result, in which case veterinary penalties will be given, or, if severe enough, the horse will be withdrawn during the ride or eliminated at the end as unfit to continue. Remember, a completion award depends in most instances on the horse, in theory, being able to continue unharmed should a further distance be imposed.

GATES   While teaching the horse obedience to the leg and rein teach him to obey the indirect rein. There will be many times when you will need to manoeuvre the horse by this method, at the same time using only one hand on the reins, specifically in negotiating the occasional (and on some rides very frequent) gates. It is no good just being able to neck-rein the horse over to the gate to be opened. One often sees a rider trying to persuade the horse to place himself alongside a gate and the horse is unco-operative in varying degrees. Some just will not approach the gate; some will not stand for it to be opened; yet others stand while it is being opened and then barge through, catching the rider's knee on the gate post, or getting the latch jammed in their own stomach because the gate was not opened sufficiently wide before they barged through. I have known a serious injury result because the horse did just this. The horse fidgeted, refused to wait, barged through, got the protruding catch of a gate jammed in his barrel, reacted, threw his rider who in turn broke his arm. Quite often the horse will approach the gate head on and because the rider has not taught him to yield to the leg refuses to align his body sideways to the gate. Much time is lost on rides where horses are unco-operative at gates. This has to be made up by riding just that bit harder in some other sections. In a ride with numerous gates the result is a lack of overall rhythm and extra stress put on both horse and rider.

Some gates are well hung and present no problem to the well-schooled horse. Others are either very low and on a very tall horse cannot be easily reached, or are secured by various bits of wire or binder twine. It is always quicker to dismount and deal with these, opening the gate sufficiently wide so that the horse gets through safely. The horse must have been taught to stand stock still for remounting. It is dangerous, and time consuming, to have a horse jiggling about and trying to rush off before given the aid to proceed by the rider. It is a very good idea to train the horse to line himself up alongside a bank or a treetrunk, or to step into a depression in the ground in order to facilitate his rider's remounting. One of my present horses who is over 16 hands is trained for this and it makes all the difference to ease and safety in remounting. If you do have an incurable barger turn him away from the way you intend going, and take your inside rein shorter so if he does move off he moves around you.

Hazards

During the course of a season's competitions you will meet many different obstacles. Get the horse used to passing all manner of strange objects: farm vehicles in all their variety, many of which appear alarming to the horse; flapping plastic; dogs yapping and threatening to attack – these are often chained and all the more aggressive and can frighten some horses. Usually a sharp word and a raised riding whip or fist will deter a loose aggressive dog, and if it does chase, turn and face it. It will almost certainly back off, particularly if the horse in turn approaches it instead of running.

For a horse unused to moving amongst farm animals it is often alarming to him to go through a field of cows. Cows are curious creatures and frequently gallop in their very ungainly fashion up to horses. This tends to alarm and unsettle the horse. A herd of sheep scattering at a horse's approach is usually more frightening to the horse than the horse is to the sheep. Whatever you do, do not go through the middle of a herd but skirt it and proceed slowly. This may seem an unnecessary caution but many horses do not have the opportunity to meet farm animals, herds or flock, in the course of their normal work. Try to give them sufficient foretaste of this before competing. Some horses are also petrified of donkeys. I do not understand why, but it is so.

WATER Many horses hate getting their feet wet. Educate them at home to go through water. Most will try to skirt puddles and often a rider allows this, not wishing to get wet either. It sets up problems later. Ride the horse through the centre of water, even small puddles. For this the horse must be controlled between hand and leg, or his front feet get wet and his hindquarters veer around the edge of the water. Introduce him to flowing water. This is sometimes almost impossible if you live in an area with no naturally flowing or accessible streams. It is well worth the extra expense and effort to go to a suitable venue prior to a competition. You will definitely meet running water during a season's events. Some horses will walk down an incline to water but are chary of stepping down even a very slight drop to it, so try to acquaint them with both aspects.

BRIDGES One meets a great variety of bridges on endurance rides, ranging from the narrow planking over a small stream to the full-flown solid wide structure. Some bridges, though wide, are definitely spooky because they bounce when crossed. Wooden ones in wet weather are very slippery. They also sometimes have a rotten core to some of the planking. Be alert for any danger in this area, though ride management should have warned competitors beforehand and should have indicated by hazard marks any unsafe section. Frequently it is only one rotten board, the rest of the bridge being safe. The two things most likely to upset a horse new to crossing bridges, particularly wooden ones, are the hollow ring as he moves across, and the gap underneath between planking and earth where the bridge

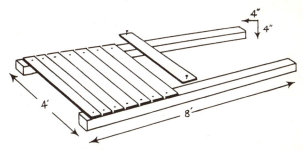

A home-made bridge to introduce the horse to hazards. Use two eight-foot 4″ × 4″ timbers, with strong planking nailed across. Four foot wide is sufficient.

rests on the cross struts. For some reason that black gap is alarming to horses.It helps to construct a simple bridge at home with two four-inch-square timbers about eight feet in length and sections of sound planking nailed across. It does not need to be any wider than four feet, even less will suffice, but it will give the horse the feel of stepping up, let him see the dark gap underneath, and hear the hollow sound as he walks across. It need not be very expensive, and it is worth the time and cost involved if you are training in an area that is bridgeless.

BOGS In certain locations favoured for annual rides because of the miles of uninterrupted access to open country and because of scenic beauty, one of the hazards is boggy ground. All such hazards should be noted in pre-ride information, but the sensible rider keeps alert. Indications of boggy ground are rank, tall, reedlike grasses, sometimes yellowish tussocky growth, and in many places very lush green growth in the midst of more normal, less verdant ground. Bog Cotton – which has a reedlike stem with a little white fluffy head like a cotton boll – is a sure warning. Bogs can start suddenly and one stride takes you right in. This is one reason for the horse being immediately responsive to the reins, as the wary rider should recognize the change before reaching a bad patch and proceed cautiously. The horse that slows down reluctantly would be up to his belly before he obeys.

Useful Habits

CIVILITY   The horse should be trained so that he will work equally well alone or in company. In company he should accept his place in the bunch, neither being unpleasant if restrained behind the current leader, nor bad tempered if a rider is close behind. However, I realize some horses react to company as if to a challenge and never settle well to second place. Although not a cure, as this is a trait hard to eradicate, I recommend consistent steady work with no spurts of speed at all. By all means cover the ground fast but consistently, not with sudden acceleration into a temporary very fast phase. This is guaranteed to act like a drug to such horses. Quite often a hard season does teach these aggravating animals to conserve their energy.

DRINKING EN ROUTE   Although not schooling per se, it is common sense to teach the horse to drink en route before you enter your season's events. One of the best ways is to be in the company of a horse used to drinking from puddles, as young horses are great copiers. Always encourage a horse to drink. Never be impatient with him even if he does not actually need the drink. He has to learn for himself and patience in training will pay dividends in later competitions, as dehydration is very dangerous and in extreme cases can be the cause of elimination. If you are in company and your horse wants to drink and your companion's horse does not ask him/her to wait while your horse drinks, as otherwise your horse will be more interested in keeping up with his friend than topping up his fluid level.

URINATING EN ROUTE It is important that the horse is allowed to urinate (stale) en route. In the course of an average day's training ride he probably will not wish to do so, but if he does, recognize the signs and allow him plenty of time to do so. Most horses that wish to stale are uncomfortable for a considerable time before they actually stop and urinate. They seem unwilling to go forward as freely, and in some cases stop frequently, sometimes even adopting a half position prior to urinating with nothing happening. Provided you are patient, and with a young horse it often takes many rides before he realizes he actually can stale while a rider is on him, he will eventually do so and once relieved pick up a forward-moving stride again. The horse that cannot stale en route sometimes gets to the stage that he will tie up and be unable to go forward at all and end up being eliminated. Do remember, though, that horses hate staling on to hard ground where they get splashed, so if your horse keeps slowing down or stopping pull him on to soft grassy ground, ease your weight forward and wait. It also helps if he exercises in company with an 'old hand' that has no inhibitions about spending pennies. As with the drinking, the young horse will frequently copy the other horse.

7 Preliminary Organization

Pre-Season Thinking

Before embarking on any training consider what you are aiming for. Is your goal a series of 25-mile rides of the pleasure and/or C.T.R. category, or do you hope to aim higher after initial introduction to the events? When do you want to enter your first competition? How much time can you devote to your new sport? How often do you intend competing? How often can you afford to compete.

The season starts by early March, B.H.S. just before, E.H.P.S. not long after, H.L.D.R.C. according to each Scottish area's climate, but some rides as early as February. At the rate the sport is growing more and more rides will come into the calendar each year. However, for climatic and light reasons early March is about the earliest sensible date. If you are entering the earlier 25-mile C.T.R. rides you should have started work with your horse a minimum of six weeks beforehand. If you have never competed in this sport before it would be better to err on the generous side and start two months before. You can then increase the distances ridden in training over a longer period of time. Do not shortchange either yourself or your horse by trying to get him fit in less than six weeks. It takes an experienced rider to assess what individual horses need, even for a 25-mile ride. Some need a longer preparation time, some can be fit for that distance in a relatively short period, but until you have considerable miles and a few seasons behind you, you will not be able to judge with any degree of accuracy. Older horses that have a few seasons' distance work under their girths already have their muscles, joints, tendons, in fact their whole frames strengthened by previous seasons and need correspondingly less initial work for the lower distance levels. They still need lengthy training for the longer, tougher rides. The horse with the slow build up will stay sound longer and withstand the eventual stresses better.

THE LOG   Keep a distance diary in which you log your daily mileage; the time taken to ride it; the type of work you do; any notable climatic conditions – for instance was it windy, humid, brisk, hot, excessively cold? All have a bearing on the results, especially the first two. In windy weather and when going against the wind considerably more energy will be used in combating it than with a similar distance ridden on a calm day. Humidity can cause elevated pulse and respiration rates, and in summer such conditions should be ridden with more than usual caution.

Occasionally note how the horse is progressing; record his pulse and respiration at the end of work and thirty minutes later. If this is done at the end of each week's schedule it will give you a good idea of his progress. If recovery is good he is achieving fitness. If poor, maybe he is slow to achieve optimum condition, or maybe something else is causing poor recovery. Is he off his feed? Is he sore in the back or in the legs? Poor recovery is an indication to look deeper for the cause than mere fatigue, as the early training distances should be insufficient to cause stress. I like to keep a weekly mileage total, and then a monthly one. Any salient points are noted – the days the horse went exceptionally well, or the reverse; his appetite; periodic heart and respiration rates; and particularly his attitude to longer rides and/ or competitions themselves. A well-kept log can be an invaluable reference book, and a help in successive seasons.

HEART AND RESPIRATION RATES   All societies have a cut-off level for the heart rate, beyond which the horse is not allowed to continue in the competition. Although it may vary slightly according to whether it is C.T.R. or E.R., nearly all rules follow the guidelines of the Fédération Equestrian Internationale (F.E.I.) with an upper limit of 64 heartbeats per minute. This is the rate to which the horse's pulse *must have dropped after thirty minutes rest*, both at any mandatory holdovers during rides and at the end of the ride. It does not matter how high the horse's pulse is on coming in at a mandatory halt or at the finish. It is the recovery to the acceptable rate that is important. Naturally, the better trained the horse and the fitter and better distance animal he is the quicker his rate will drop. It is important to ride with this thought constantly in mind. Do not spur on just before a mandatory stop. It is best to bring the horse in quietly with his heart rate already dropping nicely. Respiration is not used in any judgement, but if it indicates that trouble is brewing it will be assessed in conjunction with other factors. The fact that respiration is not used as a judgement factor is something new in the B.H.S. rules, and relatively new in the E.H.P.S., just in case any newcomers have heard the old system of judging and get confused.

The healthy, fit, distance horse will register a heart rate of between 36 and 42 beats per minute at rest. Some horses have a lower reading than others, but this is an individual characteristic and does not mean that the 36 beat horse is fitter than the 42 beat horse. The normal respiration rate at rest is between 8 and 14 per minute. Both rates rise when the horse is active, and the harder the activity the higher the rise. The heart rate approximately doubles, and in excessively arduous or fast work such as climbing precipitous hills or after a gallop the heart rate could well register triple the base rate, but it is the rapidity with which it recovers the base rate or near base rate that is important. Respiration triples or more according to effort. To monitor these rates takes a little practice but is something you should learn, and the horse be accustomed to having done. Respiration can be counted by observing the horse's flanks and counting the flank movements in and out. Each sequence of in and out means one respiration. If the horse has a double lift (that is any sort of lung problems) it will be one respiration to every three movements. I mention this because adverse respiratory conditions, although highly undesirable, do occur for a variety of reasons, and provided your veterinary surgeon is consulted and his advice followed it is quite possible to be successful with a horse that has a respiratory problem. I know this from experience. To take the heart rate a stethoscope should be placed in the girth region on the lefthand side, just about six inches back from the horse's elbow. Some horse's register a loud beat on the stethoscope, some a quieter one, but it is the regular two-beat rhythm that is

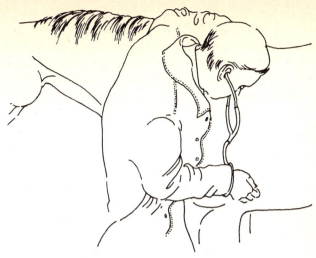

Checking heart rate. At first it can be difficult to find the correct spot, and the horse should learn to stand still both for you and for the vet.

important, not the volume. It takes a bit of practice to identify and the horse should stand very still. Any movement makes the rate rise, or the person listening lose the place, which means starting over again. Take it over a minute if possible. Short readings can be used for a quick monitoring, but accuracy needs the full minute. Pulse readings can also be taken at any pulse point on the horse's body using the finger tips placed very lightly over the pulse and counting. The best place for such a reading is under the jaw, and/or behind the knee. Practice until you are used to doing it, but a horse that fidgets about makes this type of reading very difficult to use.

Planning the Season

The main societies have a points system, fully explained in their respective rules, whereby horses accrue points over the whole season towards end-of-year awards. Although there is no upward limit to the number of rides which can be undertaken, in the E.H.P.S. only the ten best scores per horse can be counted. If you intend aiming at any end-of-season award it means an early start to your season. This allows for a bad score or two to be rejected, and for the occasional elimination. Sometimes a low score or elimination happens to the best of horses and riders, and may not even be due to anything deleterious in the horse's performance. I have ridden many types of horse in all ranges of event, but my youngest took the best part of a season before he started to get high scores and this was due solely to 'event and venue nerves'. His heart rate shot up as soon as he was at the venue, and settled beautifully on the course. Throughout ten rides in his first season he did not acquire a penalty in any other section, but he attracted heart penalties solely due to excitement. I used that season as a throwaway and by the end of the year he was responding better and his performance pleased me more than another horse who got consistently high scores merely because she was totally blasé at venues.

ACHIEVEMENT IN MODERATION   If you hope to place in the annual awards it means starting training no later than mid-January. Once you have your first event safely behind you look ahead, but be careful not to overload the horse with too many competitions. If he is a four- or five-year-old once every three weeks is plenty. Sometimes events will be as little as two weeks apart, sometimes as much as five, but if you competed every two weeks the tally at the end of the season would be too much for a novice and immature horse. Older horses can take more frequent events and a heavier total mileage, but even here I would not want to be campaigning a horse to his maximum. An older horse can do as many 25 milers as you please (and your pocket can stand) as when engaging in the longer competitions 25 milers can serve as a training ride, but 40 and 50 milers are best left to a monthly routine. Do not be so conservative that the horse is never stretched a little. He should be asked that little bit more all the time and a watch kept to ensure he does not go stale.

Major rides such as the Golden Horseshoe, E.H.P.S. Endurance Rides, the 100 milers and the Scottish Championships all come into their respective schedules when the season is well advanced, so training for low distance rides can dovetail nicely into the elevation to longer distances. If you elect to stick with shorter rides for a season or two, once the horse is fit he needs maintenance work, not continual conditioning.

8 Training: Judicious Preparation

Work Plan

The keynote to getting a horse fit for any level of long distance riding is consistency. Some horses take longer to get fit than others, but there is no such thing as a horse that keeps himself fit. Because of their natural ebullience some horses appear to be fitter than they are and some riders have erred in thinking these horses are capable of doing the job, especially the lower distances, with minimal preparation. These keen horses will no doubt cope with a few rides and on the surface seem none the worse, but keep to such a system and somewhere along the line that horse will run into problems, lose condition, go lame, or develop all manner of stresses because his frame was not toughened by judicious preparation.

SPEED   As the sport has increased in popularity so have the speeds that even the lower distance rides are being run at, with the exception of Novice level events. Even these are run by the B.H.S. at 6½ m.p.h. minimum speed, and by the E.H.P.S. at between 6 and 7 m.p.h., speeds that demand quite a high level of fitness. On paper they appear to be very moderate, but remember they are average speeds and it does not take much to drop below that average. In practice it will at first seem to be quite difficult to keep to the speed. Considerable distances will have to be covered many miles above the average as even a short walking section cuts the average more than you would imagine. There will be areas where it will be advisable to proceed slowly because of heavy going, or because a portion of the route will unavoidably be along a fairly busy road where caution will dictate lowering speed. Even a gate (or a succession of them) will cause a considerable drop in overall speed.

STARTING WORK It is always best if a horse comes into serious training from a rest period. I like to rest my endurance horses for a couple of months at the end of the season so they can unwind mentally and physically. Horses need holidays and a break from routine just as much as their riders. They return to their work much fresher for the break with any minor or incipient problems that the previous season may have induced cured by the rest. Riders also relish a period where they are not compelled to turn out almost every day to ride whatever the weather. I usually bring the horse I intend campaigning (or two if I want a back-up horse) into work just after Christmas. If you are aiming at 25 milers, six weeks' training means you can start around mid-January. If you are going for 40 milers then early January is the latest you should start. If on the other hand you are not competitive yourself and just want to experience the sport under more favourable conditions you can start later and delay your first actual competition until more beneficent days arrive. But for the enthusiast I have assumed a season starting with the first rides.

The Timetable: First Weeks

No matter what the eventual distance you intend competing at the initial work is much the same. For the first couple of weeks it is quite sufficient to ride on four days of the week and all work should be kept moderate, with a lot of walking interspersed with increasing amounts of trotting. Weekdays will present the most problems to the majority of riders as the exercise sessions will have to be fitted in for some around work times, so keep the two midweek days to an hour each, and do the longer rides at the weekends when you can choose the best time.

For those who can organize their days to suit themselves – those who have flexible hours, or work from home – weekdays present fewer problems, but for the 9-to-5 worker weekday exercising means either an early morning or an after-work session. One friend of mine rides out at 5 a.m. each morning, but each individual will have to work out their own mid-winter weekday schedule to their own best advantage.

SAFETY If you have access to a riding arena use it for the shorter sessions, because for the first few weeks' work there will be times when some horses will have to be ridden in the dark, or near dark, and hazards should be minimized as much as possible. Of course there are many riders fortunate enough to have access to good open riding country, but for a large percentage of our riders much training has to be done using the local roads. Even those with reasonable access to good bridlepaths may have to ride the first and last sections of their home routes along roads before they reach their open country. If you are one of these ensure you are equipped with safeguards – a fluorescent tabard, a stirrup light, and for the horse maybe fluorescent leg bandages.

ALTERNATIVE EXERCISE POSSIBILITIES One day of the early midweek sessions could be done at home exercising the horse on the lunge rein. If you do this the daylight factor is not so important. Look into the possibilities of using an indoor arena on an occasional basis. Team up with a group of friends to share the cost of hiring an indoor school. At weekends most riding schools utilize their facilities to capacity, but during the weekdays they may well be willing, and appreciate the chance, to hire out their facilities.

APPORTIONING TRAINING Do not try to make up for curtailed midweek riding by excessively long weekend rides. For the first couple of weekends when the horse is still relatively soft and unfit one and a half to two hours slow riding on both days is sufficient. During that time he should be made to stride out to the best of his ability at the walk, and any trotting should be at a moderate, steady speed. Do not try to cover the ground at the mile-eating trot developed by the very fit endurance horse yet, please! If you cover around 20 to 25 miles a week for the first couple of weeks your horse will be receiving gentle but sufficient exercise for the first stages. Weekdays could be using between 8 to 10 miles of this and the weekends the balance.

51

LUNGEING   If you elect to lunge the horse on one day half an hour is plenty, as this is more concentrated exercise than if the horse were being ridden slowly. At this stage of training it should be conducted at moderate speed. You are toning his muscles, and starting his work programme, not trying to put him under any sort of pressure with a high level output. About 3 miles will be covered in early lungeing sessions.

Weeks Three and Four

For the third and fourth week you may still stick to a four-day week schedule. Five would be better but it may be delayed if you are finding it exceptionally difficult to cope with the lack of daylight riding time. More can be asked of the horse in the third and fourth weeks. The midweek days can still be easy, covering around 5 miles of ridden work each day, with a little increase in pace on the day you lunge the horse if you choose this as part of your schedule – maybe make this the fifth day. At weekends you can aim to cover slightly more mileage and introduce lengthier periods of trotting. Ride for a minimum of two hours on both Saturday and Sunday and lengthen the total weekly mileage to 30 or thereabouts. Do not do any speed work at all at this stage. Any cantering should be of moderate to slow type.

By this stage if the horse has a thick coat he should have been clipped. Much condition can be lost if a horse has a consistently damp sweaty coat which will leave him uncomfortable when he ceases work for the day, the wet hair chilling and staying wet however you try to dry him off. Some horses are fortunate in having a fine coat no matter what the climate. These are usually the better bred animals and they may not need clipping at all. In all his endurance career my stallion Nizzolan never once needed clipping, starting to shed his winter coat in December of all times, and he did not lose any condition as a result of not being clipped, but I think he was an exception. He was not blanketed either, but then his stable was in a very sheltered position.

By the end of the first four weeks the horse will have covered around 100 to 120 miles in training and be ready to step up the distances covered, and more importantly the speeds at which he travels. The consistent slow work will not only have started to condition his body but will have channelled his mind to steady work. With an excitable type of horse this is very important, and with this type of horse it may well be advisable to take a longer period to build fitness, delaying any faster work for as long as possible. For the first 25-mile rides it will not be necessary, and for 40 milers only a moderate amount of speed will be used. By the time 'speed demon' is into the fast rides one hopes that consistency and obedience to the rider will override the natural tendency to explode.

The Second Month

By this time February will be well under way and there will be an appreciable difference in the length of the days. It will still be dark in the early morning and not light enough for evening riding, but it will seem that the lighter days are not too far distant. If nothing else that does have an important psychological effect on the rider who knows the lighter evenings and easier conditions for training are not many weeks away.

INCREASED ENERGY EXPENDITURE During this month the tempo of work should be stepped up and the horse asked to expend more energy during his mid-week sessions, which should now occupy three days. The proportions of walking and trotting can be reversed with the greater part of the time spent in a steady 8 to 10 m.p.h. trot so that the three rides could lengthen to around 7 miles a day. Do not change pace too frequently as that prevents a good rhythm developing. The lengthy periods of trotting – 2 or 3 miles at a stretch – serve to increase lung capacity and toughen the limbs so they can sustain longer periods of work. The heart rate will rise in steady work, and with increased work the young horse's heart muscle will begin to develop to its full capacity. If no pressure is put on the horse development will not proceed. Another benefit of sustained paces, either walking, trotting or cantering, is that less energy will be spent than with a constant chopping and changing, and the horse will become more settled in his attitude to the work, not wastefully fidgeting to be off all the time.

With three of the five workdays covering a total of approximately 20 miles, the weekend sessions should be extended in both time and distance, and in increased output. Because of lack of time midweek rides now have to be ridden moderately sharply, so take at least one of the two days at weekends to do a slow ride of at least three hours, averaging around 5 m.p.h.

THE WEIGHT-BEARING FACTOR   Long distance riding has two major aspects. The first is automatically recognized by its title, but the other aspect is often overlooked. The horse has to become accustomed to carrying a rider for long periods of time, and this in itself presents an added stress. Quite often the rider too finds the extended hours in the saddle a considerable strain, particularly with rides that have to be ridden at relatively slow rates. This is because in an endurance ride where very high speeds are being produced the rider's main concentration is on maintaining fast forward movement, and this usually effectively blots out the rider's fatigue. It is when these rides cease that the rider realizes what a toll it has taken of him/her. However, on shorter rides where the speed will in all probability be only half that at which a 50-mile Endurance Ride is run, rider fatigue will not be subjugated, but may cause the rider to ride less efficiently and make the horse burn up more energy than is necessary. For these dual reasons – to accustom both horse and rider to extended riding periods – it is important that once the horse has his initial early training weeks behind him he is asked for sustained, steady effort spread over many hours. His muscles, tendons, skin over the back, and where equipment is in contact will have slowly become used to increasing work and able to sustain the added effort.

The other day at weekends can be used to give the horse extended sessions of continual trotting, but still at a moderate speed. In his midweek workouts there will not have been much time to do this as it will take part of the ride to warm up and the last mile to unwind, which will not leave much in between for any sustained effort. In riding a 10-mile distance you can utilize 8 miles, split into say two parts, to maintain a good moving on gait at approximately 10 to 12 m.p.h. The sustained effort will toughen legs and improve lung capacity. The first and last miles will be warm up and wind down periods.

CHANGE OF SCENE   Towards the sixth week consider taking the horse to a different location to do one of the lengthier training rides. If possible avail yourself of a suitable pleasure ride, if offered in your area. Pleasure rides are often the first events of a season and some shorter 15- to 20-mile rides are sometimes offered prior to the first competitive events of the season. They give the horse the chance to become accustomed to all but the extended distance, and give the rider the chance to assess how the horse will react when at his first competitive ride.

A CAUTION   One word of caution about pleasure rides. At one time they were truly pleasurable and ideal for introducing young and/or inexperienced horses to the long distance scene. They were run at conservative speeds, usually with a ride leader who set the pace and knew the route, so there was no need for markers. Riders therefore rode at a controlled speed. Many pleasure rides are now run over a marked course where the riders set off either singly or in groups and there is no upward speed limit, although there is often a 5 m.p.h. minimum average speed. Some riders consider the pleasure to be solely theirs, ruining the ride for those who wish to take it slowly. If you have a horse that is impressionable and/or excitable it would be wise to go with a friend on a really wise, steady horse, or alternatively ask that you be given a late starting time so you do not have the gangs of inconsiderate riders charging up behind.

The B.H.S. L.D.R.G. offers many training rides, particularly in the early part of the season, usually as an additional class where competitive rides are being held. The E.H.P.S. invariably has a pleasure ride amongst the classes offered at a competitive event, and the H.L.D.R.C. also offers a variety of pleasure rides. These pleasure rides are safer to enter as the individual society's rules apply to all events. It is where rides are run by inexperienced individuals or groups not conversant with long distance ride procedure that mayhem sometimes results.

Many riding clubs offer pleasure rides on a very occasional basis, and there are sponsored rides run throughout the year. It is worth a telephone call to the organizer to ask how many entrants are expected, and if there is a special group for those wanting to ride at a slow speed. Use a pleasure ride to teach the horse what is expected of him. Many pleasure rides are run on an annual basis and previous rides offer a good guide to the newcomer, so do your homework.

TRIAL RUN Throughout the second month of training you should have been gradually stepping up the total distance asked of your horse. By the last two weeks of this month the horse should be nearing low distance competition fitness. During the seventh, or at latest eighth, weekend do a simulated ride over 20 miles at the speed you intend tackling the actual competition at. See if you can successfully work out the paces you need to do and come in at a time you have set yourself. Note the horse's reaction, and also his recovery time after he has finished. How long does it take him to come down to his pre-activity heart rate? It will probably drop closer to normal level at home than it will on the first ride, unless he is a horse that is very very calm or has had previous experience of an equine social life – showing, hunter trials, or other activity.

If the horse comes through your home test well – good recovery, clean legs, with no filling after work has ceased and he has stood in the stable for a few hours; if his appetite is keen and he is drinking well; if his sweat is thin and clear, not viscous and sticky – then he is ready for competition. If there is any shortfall in any department you still have time to do the toning up needed before the actual competition. Any further training before a 25-mile ride will be of maintenance variety, unless you have elected to give him the bare seven to eight week programme. At the end of two months a 25-mile ride should present no problem to a fit horse who should be able to clip it off with plenty of reserve left so that he could, if asked, do a further 10 miles or so with no untoward effect.

The Third Month

If you are planning a 40-mile event considerable work still remains to be done. The first half of this month is where you will put the finishing touches to a horse doing a 40-mile C.T.R. or a B.H.S. Qualifier. Take in a 25-mile C.T.R. as part of your training for 40 milers if it is at all possible from the financial and travel point of view. You then have the veterinary surgeon's assessment as well as your own. After that, instead of resting the horse for a week you will have to proceed with the last stages of 40-mile training. By all means give him a couple of days off, particularly if there has been a long journey as well as the 25-mile competition.

As the rider and probably driver you will welcome the break as well.

Increase distances ridden in midweek workouts so that you are covering around 25 miles total over the three days. By now daylight saving time will have started, making midweek sessions easier and with the spring equinox close there will be more light in the mornings as well. Out of midweek sessions one day could be very moderate with 5 or 6 miles done slowly, and the other two days ridden more sharply. Mid-week times taken should now be around one and a half hours a day. You will probably only have two more weekends before you enter your first 40 miler, so do a 15-mile slow ride one day and then a 20-mile ride at a slightly faster speed than you will be required to ride at in the actual competition. At least once before the 40 miler, and a minimum of one week away from it, do a 32-mile (approximately) ride averaging a minimum of 8 m.p.h. Monitor as for the trial ride you did prior to your first 25 miler.

Do not ride at excessive speed for the Qualifying or C.T.R. type of rides. Many leg ailments occur from excessive and unnecessary speeds; speed is best left to the Endurance Ride specialists. Do not be alarmed if your horse's pulse and respiration are very high after a 30-mile plus workout. They should be relatively high, but they should also drop rapidly to normal or near normal. If they do not drop satisfactorily on several successive occasions when you monitor the horse a word with your veterinary surgeon is advisable. A heart rate in the high 80s is perfectly acceptable. In the fit horse it will have dropped to the 50s or thereabouts in ten minutes and then come down more slowly to the base rate of the low 40s in the next fifteen minutes.

9 Competition Preliminaries

When joining the B.H.S. L.D.R.G., members will be sent their annual book containing rules and a complete list of competitive rides for the forthcoming season. E.H.P.S. members are sent a Competitors' Reference Book which details all aspects of the Society's competitions. Especially interesting to a newcomer to the sport are the guidelines for veterinary surgeons adjudicating at events. These tell participants exactly how the veterinary surgeons are going to appraise horses entered in rides. Any amendments to E.H.P.S. rules are noted in the society's newsletters, so riders are kept abreast of any changes. For non-members entering E.H.P.S. rides there is always an up-to-date Competitors' Reference Book available at the ride venue so a check can be made on any points riders are uncertain about. Each E.H.P.S. newsletter carries a list of forthcoming rides. Most of the season's events are listed in the first issue out after Christmas, but there are regular additions throughout the season. All are noted well in advance and give riders ample opportunity to add a new ride to their own selection should they so wish.

The B.H.S. list of events has the closing date for entries at the top of each page carrying that particular ride's details. Also shown are the entry fees for each class scheduled. Most ride entries close approximately two weeks before the ride date, but entries for certain major events close three to four weeks before the ride, and other rides also show some variance from the two week cut-off, so do check the small print. Ride entry fees do vary within the category offered so check carefully to see just how much each ride entry fee is going to be. The longer the ride the higher the entry fee is the general rule.

The E.H.P.S. schedule of events carries the address of the

organizer/secretary, and the standard practice is to request an entry form from the organizer, at the same time enclosing a stamped addressed envelope for it to be sent. Entries usually close two weeks before the event, but with major rides, particularly the 100 miler, they close a little sooner. Entry fees are fixed at the beginning of the year and are the same throughout the country, no matter who is the organizer. Pleasure rides carry the lowest fee; C.T.R.s of all distances are the same price but higher than pleasure rides; Endurance Rides are also a standard price with the exception of the 100 miler which is considerably higher, though still very good value for money considering the amount of organization that goes into the event. Non-members may compete at a higher entry fee in all E.H.P.S. rides.

Scrutiny of the Schedule

Whichever ride you are entering read the ride schedule carefully. Some rides have overnight stabling available at the venue. Others have a list of people who are willing to put up horses (and sometimes riders) overnight and leave the individual to make the necessary arrangements. Other ride schedules advise those desiring stabling and accommodation to contact the ride secretary. All rides that use a racecourse as a venue have stabling available, and horses entered in the major classes where they are obliged to be in stables the night before, and sometimes the night after a ride, will be stabled on site. At these events there is usually ample stabling to accommodate horses in lower distance events as overnight stabling, though not obligatory, is often needed when competitors have travelled a long distance to a ride. Some racecourses also have stable lads' accommodation available for a nominal fee for the human element of the ride. At all racecourse venues competitors must produce evidence of up-to-date equine influenza vaccinations in order to comply with Jockey Club Rules.

When entries are sent in competitors are informed of their number, vetting and starting times, and sent a map of the course plus any other information the organizer considers helpful. Directions to the ride venue usually accompany this, but may be contained in the ride schedule sent earlier. If the course map is clear and very detailed, note can be made of access points where your 'crew' or helper (if you have one) can meet you. If the map is an Ordnance Survey one, contours will be shown for hilly country: the closer together the contours are the steeper the going. This foreknowledge will also help you plan where to ride slowly and where to make time up.

Once I have all the ride 'literature' I make out a card with road numbers, and directions to the venue, and calculate how long it will take to drive there. Allow longer than you need to take care of diversions, and any other setback you may encounter. In practice I have found that I can work out fairly accurately how long all but the last 10 miles will take. Because many ride venues are tucked away on some kind property owner's land, and the venue has been loaned for the day, it will not always be easy to find, and the last few miles could well be down winding lanes where you will have to drive slowly in order not to overshoot a turn. It is sometimes extremely difficult to turn a box around in a narrow lane if you do overshoot. Directional ride markers indicating the location of the venue will only be put up a mile or so, and sometimes not even that, before the venue. And a word of warning. Some organizers fail to realize that when one is driving and keeping one's mind on the job of driving it is impossible to see a faint, small inked direction to the venue. Unfortunately there is a percentage of directional marking that leaves much to be desired in the way of size and clarity. At all events, plan to try to arrive at least one hour before you actually start the ride.

Pre-Ride Planning

Make sure your vehicle(s) – box, car/Landrover and trailer – are in good order. Fill up with petrol (or diesel) the night before. Carry a spare can of petrol, and a container of water for the water tank. If the ride is on a Sunday when some petrol stations are closed make sure you do not let the petrol gauge drop too low. Check tyre pressures. Load the vehicle the night before with all the equipment likely to be needed, and in the order that you will need it, so that time is saved at the venue.

LISTS Make lists of all the items you are likely to need on a ride. There will be two main groups:

Items for the Horse
Saddle with fittings.
Bridle.
Numnah, or saddle pad if a Western saddle is used (and a spare numnah for changing at each mandatory stop. These spares are not essential on short distance rides, but on longer ones are very useful, particularly if it is hot and the horse sweaty).
Spares – extra girth, numnahs as above, reins, leathers, irons, halter and lead.
Coolers – a lightweight one for hot weather, and a heavier one for colder days or the sudden temperature changes to which we are liable in Britain.
Spare rug. On soaking wet days a spare is useful as there is a wait between when you finish the ride and when you present the horse to the veterinary surgeon for post-ride examination, and once soaked you will need the replacement rug.
Spare set of horseshoes and nails.
Farrier's rasp (for bevelling shoe edges). An old wood rasp will do if you do not have the former.
Full grooming kit – soft and stiff brushes, hoof pick (have one attached to the saddle as well), cactus cloth (if I had to choose only one item of grooming kit this would be it, as at a pinch fingers can do manes and tails and a stick substitute for a lost hoofpick), sponge(s).
Stethoscope and first aid kit (for horse and rider).
Two buckets – one for drinking water, one for wash water.
Electrolytes and salt for the longer distance rides.
One small sack of sawdust (not shavings) to encourage a horse to stale. Most horses do this freely, but others that retain urine will need some encouragement and some definitely will not go unless on an absorbent patch of grass, or the sawdust. I once owned a horse that would not go until he was put back in the trailer.
Sharp knife – useful if a horse panics for any reason while tied. One quick cut and he is safe. This should not happen but on occasion it does.
Water container (5 gallon). If you are doing a very long ride take correspondingly more.
Short-handled shovel (keep in a plastic sack) for clearing droppings from trailer.

Filled haynet with enough to last out and return trip.
A short feed if the return trip is likely to be very late.

Items for the Human

Riding gear and a complete change of clothing, including under-
wear, socks and shoes. It is not at all comfortable travelling
home in soaking wet clothes.

Gloves. Control of the horse is difficult with wet slippery reins,
and on a cold early season ride frozen hands refuse to operate
efficiently.

Sustenance for after the ride. Some rides have good catering
facilities but refreshments are usually of the 'fast food' variety
and it is easier to have some of your own ready packed. Cheaper too! Take plenty of fluids, especially for hot weather riding.
Your crew will do double duty dishing out drinks to horse and
rider.

Carry in a pocket: loose change for a telephone call; a sterile pad
or clean handkerchief and a bandage (useful for horse and/or
rider); a piece of string (for a quick repair job out on the trail, or
for a temporary hold together). The lot takes hardly any room.

THE NIGHT BEFORE   Lay out all you will need ready to hand for
kitting the horse out for travelling.

Blanket. If it is cold use it. If it is warm do not, as it can get quite hot
in a trailer or horsebox. It will probably be cooler on the return trip
if it is late, and if the horse is tired he can chill easily and also
stiffen up. Guard against this with a blanket. On the other hand if
it is sweltering on the return trip do not rug up. Use common
sense.

Leg wraps. I prefer the type fastening with velcro, then I can easily
make sure that they cover the horse's coronet completely. They
go on quickly and are removed equally so. Some horses are
bandaged before travelling but the vital coronet and lower pastern area is left unprotected and that is one of the most vulnerable
parts of the horse's legs. If you use bandages with ties make sure
they are done up on the outside of the leg with no tapes left
dangling that could get stepped on, causing unravelling and
consequent panic if the horse gets tangled in them. It may seem

unnecessary to offer this caution but I have seen people bandage this way with tapes on the inside.

Tail bandage. It is a good idea to take a clean, already rolled one for the return journey.

Persuaders. If you have an awkward loader take whatever is necessary to persuade him to reload on the homeward trip. Horses that are less than perfect in this area are always at their worst away from home. They are either determined to see what is happening around them; or they are certain that coercion will not be as positive away from home base. An owner is doing his horse a disservice if he refrains from positive action, as the crafty horse quickly gets impossible and has to be taken to task even more strongly. Regardless of what the 'never hit your horse, he doesn't understand' school of thought says it is quite obvious that these horses do understand only too well. There are many ways of persuading the horse to box other than hitting him, which is usually the last and unsuccessful resort, other than a swift crack at a crucial moment. An iron fist in the velvet glove, or determination coupled with a quiet manner, works well.

OVERNIGHT STABLING   If you are putting your horse in rented stabling you will probably be given a choice of bedding. However, I have been caught (only once, fortunately), having the requested type of bedding supplied but in such a minimal quantity that the horse did not relax at all overnight. It is a ticklish subject. If you mention *plenty* of bedding it implies a criticism (and people are too ready to take offence). If you do not request plenty you may get caught out. If at all possible when going to a venue you do not know take a top up reserve and use if needed. A hammer is also useful as many places have unsafe protrusions in stables – nails, loose boards, and so on. Take sufficient hay and feed to last, and if staying just one night it should be possible to take sufficient water. A few horses do not like 'strange' water and will not drink adequately. Dehydration can be one of the worst enemies on a long distance ride.

Arriving at the Venue

Arrive at the venue well in advance of your vetting time. I like to arrive one hour ahead, and, as I often travel solo, not always having the luxury of a friend to crew, I have to organize things efficiently. However, one of the nice things about long distance riding is that there is always a helping hand at venues, and often en route as well, for those without help. But do plan so you can cope alone.

On arrival I always do things in sequence: get my number, spend a penny, return to the trailer and unload all the equipment I need, and then untie the horse while the tailgate of the trailer is still up. Once that is lowered the horse is told to back out. If he gets bargy about unloading a good swat on the rump prefaces the dropping of the tail gate, or even the stiff bristles of a broom. It is far better to do this than risk an accident. He should have had some home training on this score, and refreshers when necessary. Horses are not always the most obliging of creatures, and safety comes before being considered 'sweet to your horse'. It will not do you much good if you get knocked down and injured because you were too lenient with discipline. Many horses are co-operative and very agreeable characters, but just as many have less than desirable sides to their behaviour and this is tolerated far too often.

Once unloaded attend to the horse calmly, removing his travelling 'clothes'. I do not approve of tying a horse to the trailer. Too much is happening around him. I prefer him to stand while I attend to him (again prior training), and I have a long enough lead rope so I can hold him while attending to the back end.

PRE-RIDE VETTING After unloading and settling the horse take him to the vetting area. This is, or should be, set aside from the general activity of the arrivals and departures of competing horses. The horse will be examined by the presiding veterinary surgeon(s) who will take his pulse, check his respiration, and have the rates noted on the horse's score sheet. The heart rate will be used in further judging and marked deviation from his initial resting rate will be penalized accordingly. The E.H.P.S. has a table of such penalties. The respiration is not used in adjudicating. After the heart rate is noted the horse is checked for 'lumps and bumps', that is any lesions, swellings or abrasions on his back, limbs, mouth, and so on. Any already present are examined and if not of any account the horse is allowed to proceed. If they cause, or are likely to cause, concern they are noted for

Trotting up for the vet: the right way. The horse is moving in a straight line with his head free, and is not obscured by the handler.

Trotting up for the vet: the wrong way. The horse is moving at an angle, and the handler is interfering with his head, as well as obscuring the vet's view.

future reference. The last stage of pre-ride vetting is the examination of gait. The horse will be walked and trotted away from and towards the veterinary surgeon at his request. The rider must run the horse up on a loose rein and not obscure the veterinary surgeon's view of the horse by running in front of it. The horse should have been taught to move in a straight line, not veer all over the place. He should also move freely, not need to be dragged into an unwilling trot.

The rider has a chance during the pre-ride veterinary examination to declare any peculiarities of gait, back sensitivity, acquired blemishes, especially any fresh ones, so that the horse will not be penalized at a later stage for something not arising during the course of the ride.

TACK INSPECTIONS   All B.H.S. rides have a tack inspection prior to the start. Any defective tack must be replaced or adequately repaired.

THE FARRIER   Before starting en route horses are presented to the farrier for a shoe inspection. Horses are not allowed to start unless their shoes and hooves are in good condition, so do not present the horse with risen clenches or badly worn shoes. The ride farrier is there to check shoes and replace any shoes accidently lost. He will put new shoes on but only when this does not interfere with the duties for which he has been engaged.

VETERINARY OR SHOEING COSTS   Any expense incurred for veterinary treatment administered during the course of an event has to be borne by the individual rider. The rider will also have to pay the farrier for any shoeing services. The veterinary surgeons are at rides in an adjudicating capacity and only treat horses in an emergency situation, while the farrier only attends to inspections and emergencies.

TACKING UP   The final stage is to tack the horse up, putting the bridle on first while maintaining control with the halter secured round the horse's neck until the bridle is buckled in place. Then put the saddle on. Too many people put the saddle on first with occasional disastrous results as the horse, maybe startled, takes off around the venue minus bridle. If the horse is of a nervous disposition it would be better to bridle him in the trailer and put the halter back on over this, for then you have better control once he is unloaded. Under B.H.S. L.D.R.G. rules the horse can be presented for vetting with a bridle or a halter on. Under E.H.P.S. rules the horse must be presented in a headcollar, but one can ask for the horse to be presented in a bridle. In practice this is never refused.

THE TIMEKEEPER   Before starting en route report to the official ride timekeeper who will time the horse out. All horses must pass through the official start and finish to qualify for an award.

10 Riding the Route

Stewards and Checkpoints

All ride routes, whether they are in the C.T.R. or E.R. category, have ride stewards stationed at intervals along the course. These places are indicated on the route map by the sign 'Checkpoint 1, 2, 3' and so on. They are usually sited at road junctions to facilitate safe crossings, and also because these are easily accessible for stewards' vehicles. Competitors must go through each checkpoint and be ticked off the checkpoint steward's list. Failure to do this usually incurs elimination.

An approximate distance can be worked out between checkpoints. I say 'approximate' because the maps do not really allow for the intricacies of route windings, but they do give a fairly good guide. Checkpoint stewards should know how many miles they are from the start, and from the course finish. Some do, but it has been my experience that many do not know, so it is important that the rider does not rely on a steward for accurate information. Some, while hazarding a guess, are doing just that, and I have been told by at least three successive and closely spaced stewards that they were all the same number of miles from the finish, and even then they were all miles out. Nothing beats your own homework.

AVERAGE SPEEDS A newcomer to the sport must remember that it is the average speed that is important. On E.H.P.S. rides, as long as the ride is accomplished within the time allotted for the distance, you may choose your own speed and elect to do the first portion of the route somewhat faster than the last. On B.H.S. rides it is frequently the case that each section of the ride must be covered at the minimum average speed required for the whole distance. For example, if a B.H.S. ride has a stipulated speed of 7 m.p.h. minimum average, then a 10-mile section, the likely distance between checkpoints, must take no more than one hour, twenty-six minutes. It may be ridden faster, as the B.H.S. rides always stipulate the lowest speed at which the route may be ridden. On an E.H.P.S. ride a similar 10-mile section may be ridden at less than the 7 m.p.h. average, provided that the overall distance is ridden at the required speed. E.H.P.S. C.T.R. rides always have a minimum and a maximum speed laid down. This is rather more difficult to attain as it does need close monitoring of averages and a sensible approach to riding the whole course. Of the two I prefer the E.H.P.S. system, especially as the rider may still earn a completion even if outside the perfect time score, penalty points being deducted at the rate of one point for every three minutes or part of three minutes up to a maximum of twenty time penalties before elimination on a time basis. On a B.H.S. ride, if you are slower than the average laid down elimination follows. However, the B.H.S. offer increasingly more difficult categories so a newcomer has plenty of opportunity to learn how to manage the time element before attempting a faster event.

Sensible Riding

Far too many horses start a ride as if they were in a hotly contested endurance race and under the false assumption that the first few minutes are going to determine the eventual winner.

With any horse, and especially with an impressionable youngster, it is important to take the first section slowly. It gives the horse time to get his muscles warmed up before asking for more strenuous effort. It helps to settle him mentally if he is expected to conduct himself calmly. It sets the pattern for future obedience. It also helps conserve physical and mental energy.

I have two horses who are totally different in character. One is of a slightly nervous disposition and gets very excited at ride starts, but is also of an obedient nature and relies on the rider to give him confidence. After half a mile of walking, in which he calms himself, he is then quite relaxed and does not mind going in company, solo, in the middle, first or last in a group. Nor does he mind another rider overtaking provided that rider does not crash up behind as unfortunately is far too prevalent nowadays. The other horse is very different. Not a nervous flicker anywhere, but not so easy or pleasurable to ride as she looks for any opportunity to forge ahead, cannot stand another rider in front, and any horse overtaking is not to be borne. Consequently she will burn up a lot of nervous energy as well as giving her rider a few hair-raising moments. Her home preparation entails a lot of discipline, and much slow work to settle her head as much as conditioning her body. For the first miles I can feel the resentment in her whole body when she is restrained, but finally she will relax and forget her sulks. The other horse's home work is a lot easier as he is much like his father, my stallion Nizzolan, and he does not even need the overt discipline as he happily co-operates, so that the end result is that sometimes I choose the pace, sometimes he does. However, he never takes liberties, whereas the mare most certainly would.

Thus the way you ride the course will depend to a great extent on the mental approach of your horse.

COMPANIONSHIP If you have travelled with a companion whose horse is also entered in the same class your partnership problems are settled. For those who arrive alone the chances of riding with someone else are very good, and will probably give the horse new to the sport a definite help on his first few rides. There are usually quite a few riders who are in the same position and would welcome riding the 25 miles (or 40 if you are being adventurous) in company. They are probably the ones who ride solo at home and hope for a change at competitions. However, a word of caution. It is always politic to enquire what speed section your prospective partner is entered in. If in the same category fine. Also enquire what plan he/she has for riding the route. I would far rather ride alone than have to go with a 'hare and tortoise' companion. One who is prepared to keep a steady pace with no rushed sections is by far the best. Naturally it is of help if the 'new equine friends' are of similar size with a reasonably matched stride. It is not a good idea to team up with a horse that is cavorting about and quite obviously not under complete control. Such antics are definitely infectious, unless your horse is of a decidedly placid and unperturbable nature.

Speed En Route

Aim to ride the whole route just a little faster than the minimum required speed (according to whichever society's rules you are competing under). That gives you a cushion of spare time to fall back on if something untoward should happen. It also allows you to do the last section at a more moderate speed. Even with the rides where each section has to be ridden at the minimum average careful planning will allow you to do the last mile or so at a slower rate. Start the ride circumspectly. Take your time and get the horse well settled before you forge ahead. If you wish it

Allowing the horse to take care of himself, and incidentally you, over very difficult going.

is quite in order to start at a moderate trot, providing it is controlled. It will take about a mile to get into a really good rhythm. It is important to maintain a steady pace for relatively long stretches of the route. Much energy is wasted if you constantly slow down and speed up for short spurts. It unsettles the horse, cuts your overall average, and makes any ground-eating stride almost impossible to establish.

Allow the horse as much freedom from rein restraint as possible. He will be learning how to cope with strange territory and possibly different and difficult underfoot conditions. He will not learn to become efficient if you constantly hold him up. Hopefully your prior training sessions will pay off here. The long distance horse should be a thinking equine, able to take care of himself (and you) over pretty rough going. If you constantly pick at him he will never gain the confidence to do so.

When trotting remember to change your diagonal every mile or so in order to give both sides of the horse equal work. On a 25

Not enough freedom: going uphill. This horse cannot use himself fully.

72

miler it will not make that much difference, but on very long rides it could be very important. I have known horses pull up lame on 100 milers where only one diagonal was used. When cantering alternate the horse's leads for the same reason. Get into these habits and later they will become automatic.

When you come to any lengthy stretch of good level going make use of it by travelling faster, but still under control. It is the rare ride that does not have some section where the horse will have to be ridden well under the average speed.

ROADWORK   Nearly all routes have a percentage of roadwork. Where the map shows these to be of fairly short duration it would be best to allow the horse to walk. He can recoup his energies ready for the next piece of natural going, and it is far safer walking on a road than trotting. At home you will have got to know patches of road that afford good traction and those that are slippery. Another reason I dislike trotting on the roads is the concussive effect on the horse's legs and joints. Horses were not designed to pound over unyielding surfaces, and I feel they stay sounder longer if that hammering is avoided as much as poss-ible. Many riders trot far too fast and hard on roads. On courses with considerable portions alongside roads it is possible to use even the narrowest verge if the horse is well schooled. In using these do pay attention to where you are going. Motorists tend to throw rubbish out of car windows so the verge closest to the road is usually the worst endowed where there is a litter prob-lem. Most verges are safe, especially those along minor and little-used lanes. Watch for drainage ripples in verges, particu-larly in high summer where they could be overgrown with long grass. I do pay particular attention at home over this and the horses get into trouble if they do not look where they are going. They do soon learn to cope with all but the worst of the drainage cuts, nipping cleverly over them without any appreciable break in gait rhythm.

MONITORING DISTANCE   At home you will have had all your training sessions to learn to recognize when you have ridden a mile. It will pay dividends in actual competition as you will be able to keep a rough check on your progress. However, do not expect to be dead accurate. Different locations do upset calcula-

Time (hours, minutes, seconds) required to cover a certain distance at a given speed

Distance	Speed					
	5 m.p.h.	6 m.p.h.	7 m.p.h.	8 m.p.h.	9 m.p.h.	10 m.p.h.
1 mile	12 m	10 m	8 m 36 s	7 m 30 s	6 m 40 s	6 m
5 miles	1 h	50 m	43 m	37 m 30 s	33 m 20 s	30 m
10 miles	2 h	1 h 40 m	1 h 26 m	1 h 15 m	1 h 6 m 40 s	1 h
20 miles	4 h	3 h 20 m	2 h 52 m	2 h 30 m	2 h 13 m 20 s	2 h
25 miles	5 h	4 h 10 m	3 h 33 m 44 s	3 h 7 m 30 s	2 h 46 m 40 s	2 h 30 m
30 miles	6 h	5 h	4 h 17 m 12 s	3 h 45 m	3 h 20 m	3 h
35 miles	7 h	5 h 50 m	5 h	4 h 22 m 30 s	3 h 53 m 20 s	3 h 30 m
40 miles	8 h	6 h 40 m	5 h 43 m	5 h	4 h 26 m 40 s	4 h
50 miles	10 h	8 h 20 m	7 h 8 m 36 s	6 h 15 m	5 h 33 m 20 s	5 h
75 miles	15 h	12 h 30 m	10 h 43 m	9 h 22 m 30 s	8 h 20 m	7 h 30 m
100 miles	20 h	16 h 40 m	14 h 17 m 12 s	12 h 30 m	11 h 6 m 40 s	10 h

These times are to the nearest second and do not allow for any mandatory stops, time taken for these having to be added to the total.

tions, but it will assist you in keeping to the average speed. At each checkpoint you can re-estimate how you are doing and increase or decrease your speed accordingly. A word of caution on this point. Away from home it nearly always seems that you have covered more ground than you actually have, so do not be lulled into a false sense of security. Do remember that checkpoint stewards, even if they are reasonably sure of how far they are from ride base, will only give you a 'guesstimate' to the nearest mile or two. Even one mile out could be the difference between a time penalty or a perfect time score, so monitor your travel speed all the time.

Along the Way

RIDER INDEPENDENCE   Do not be influenced by what other riders are doing around you. Ride the way you, and possibly your companion, have planned. You may well be lucky enough to team up with an experienced long distance rider who is bringing a new horse out and can therefore help you and your horse on his first outing. Most experienced riders are more than willing to help newcomers, as they will recall when they needed help themselves. One of the big bonuses in C.T.R. is that when one rider helps another he/she does not jeopardize his/her horse's chances of a win in doing so, because most C.T.R.s have graded awards and theoretically all horses can achieve the top grade if their finishing condition warrants it. Naturally on an Endurance Ride those going for a win will not appreciate any rider tagging along, but the Endurance levels are still some way away in time from the newcomer.

A CAUTION WARRANTED   Having stated one of the major plusses of competitive riding I must now state the biggest disadvantage of the sport now that it has blossomed into a major equestrian activity. In its early years there was definitely more courtesy on the long distance trail. There was an unwritten code of ethics. Riders were invariably considerate towards each other. They did not gallop past a group of horses going at a more leisurely pace, but slowed down and then passed in a controlled manner. Unfortunately, as the sport has expanded there are far too many instances of 'I'm all right, Jack', and it is not uncommon to have horses out of control come barging up the back of other riders, some riders even using more controlled horses as buffers. Some horses, once in front, take off at a flat-out gallop which is definitely unsettling to young and/or inexperienced horses.

I would advise staying out of tight bunches of riders, riding only with a very few companions. If you hear a cavalry charge coming up behind you, sign to them to slow down. Failing that pull over and let them by if possible. If your horse gets upset and wants to join in or gets frightened into carting you for a little, turn him in the other direction. It will cost you a little time, but be worthwhile, and once he is settled you can then set out en route again.

In two successive seasons there have been incidents of this nature. One young girl on a novice purebred Arabian gelding got carted for a full 5 miles by an irresponsible bunch of gallopers; on another ride there were three very aggravating and ill-mannered riders who constantly galloped up behind, took off in front, and so on. Their collective excuse was 'I can't stop'. And no wonder! On the rare occasions when they did walk and then found themselves in a stubble field, they invariably urged their already ill-mannered horses into a fast gallop, only being able to pull up by circling at the other end of the fields. There has also been a very sad accident where an endurance rider has had her horse used as a buffer by a rider unable to stop, and in the process the horse in front sustained an injury that has finished her successful career.

SPOT CHECKS   On 25 milers there will be no mid-ride checks or mandatory stops, although if there are sufficient veterinary surgeons available there may well be a 'spot check' somewhere en route, most likely towards the three-quarter mark. If the ride organizer is fortunate in having a roving veterinary surgeon available he/she will merely hold each horse up for a cursory, momentary scrutiny. If satisfied the veterinary surgeon will permit the horse to proceed. If there is cause for alarm the veterinary surgeon will recommend coming in at a slower pace. Naturally if there are any lame horses these will be pulled from the ride.

DRINKING AND STALING EN ROUTE   Although this has been

more fully covered in an earlier chapter, remember that these two aspects of the horse's wellbeing could mean the difference between success and failure. Give the horse every opportunity to drink from streams, clean puddles, and so on, and be alert for signs that he wishes to urinate.

Back at Base

Aim to come into ride base very slowly. You should have ridden the last mile at a walk. This has several benefits. The horse's heart rate will be dropping nicely, and his muscles will already be beginning to relax. His frame of mind will also be calm. You must pass the timekeeper and be officially checked in. You will be told how long you have to your post-ride veterinary examination. This is usually thirty minutes after the ride finish and in that thirty minutes you will have a lot to do.

After dismounting do not immediately slacken the girth, but wait a few moments before releasing the pressure. According to the ambient temperature I may or may not put a cooler on. If it is chilly I definitely will, especially if there is a sharp wind as well and in that case the heavier type is best. If it is moderately warm I will put a lightweight one over his back, but if it is hot and sultry with no breath of air I do not put anything on the horse at all. As soon as possible remove the bridle and put his halter on. Offer the horse about half a bucket of water, preferably with the chill off. Do not feed him grain. If you wish he can pick at some hay, or if you allow it he may graze. I offer hay from a haynet. I do not let the horse graze as he then tends to wander and it is difficult to work around him while his teeth are chasing grass. It also gives him the idea he can graze any time he is not actually being ridden, as he will not differentiate the end of the ride grazing from any other time. It is an extremely annoying habit.

After a ride of 25 miles the horse should not have used so much energy that he will need walking to remain supple prior to being trotted out. If it is very chilly I will walk the horse very very slowly before presenting him to the veterinary surgeon. If it is hot he will not need it as much. (The condition changes after the longer, faster rides where more detailed care will be advisable. For a more thorough study of the sport at higher levels see Ann Hyland, *The Endurance Horse* (J. A. Allen, 1988).)

77

By the time you have removed the bridle and offered a moderate amount of water and got his cooler on, you can loosen the girth while still leaving the saddle on. I do not remove this until just before I take the horse to the veterinary surgeon for examination. In the half hour allowed between ride finish and final vetting you will only be able to make the horse moderately comfortable. Sometimes a hot horse defies all attempts to really clean him, and the veterinary surgeons do not expect a pristine, show condition horse to be presented. They do, however, expect the horse to have been made as comfortable as possible by removing the worst of the trail muck. I find the best thing to do is just remove the worst and leave the rest until he is either home or in base stables after the ride. Whatever you do, keep the horse calm in the half hour, and just prior to seeing the veterinary surgeon walk the horse *slowly* to the vetting area.

POST-RIDE VETTING The veterinary surgeon will take the horse's pulse before any other part of the examination is done. It is always taken over at least thirty seconds, and where possible over one minute. The closer it comes to the starting pulse rate the higher the mark in that category. The next section will be for trauma, that is any abrasions caused by tack, or any self-inflicted interference marks especially to the lower limbs. Pressure bumps and/or sensitive areas in the back are also examined. Finally the horse will have to be trotted out to see if he is still sound. A heart rate that has not dropped back to near its starting rate will attract a sliding scale of penalties. A rate over 64 will incur elimination in both societies. Any trauma also incur penalties and the more severe they are the more penalties they receive. If there is any cut or sore that would make it impossible for the horse to continue without damaging himself further then he is eliminated. However, in the final test for soundness in the limbs he is either sound and will pass the examination in that department, or he is not and will be eliminated for lameness. There are no degrees of lameness at present in Britain, although in some other countries there is a sliding scale for that too!

FINAL TASKS AT THE VENUE Return your number and collect the deposit paid. In the case of members riding in an E.H.P.S. event you will have surrendered your membership card and this is exchanged for the number at the end of the ride. Collect your well-earned award, together with the sheet that should tell you what, if any, penalties your horse acquired and for what reason. Look forward to the next ride in the knowledge that you and your horse have come through the first event successfully and have learnt a lot from the experience.

11 The Trip Home and After-Ride Care

Preparing for the Homeward Journey

As soon after final vetting as possible get the horse ready for the return trip home. If it is cold blanket him, and if he shows signs of fatigue an extra covering will not come amiss on a cold day. Fatigue often makes a horse feel cold even if the ambient temperature is moderate. However, if it is a sultry day and you are travelling home in daylight dispense with the blanket(s). If it is hot and you will be doing the bulk of the homeward trip after the heat of the day has gone put a thin blanket on. He will not sweat to start with, unless it is excessively hot, but he will need the light covering when the temperature drops. Offer a final drink before loading, or maybe after loading just before setting off. He probably will not need it, particularly if you have already made sure his fluid levels are maintained, but it will be a long time before unloading. I prefer to keep moving rather than stop on the way home.

Home Care

Once you are home it is better to turn the horse out in a paddock for a short time so he can stretch his legs and get rid of any travel stiffness. Although he will have done a considerable number of long training rides, the added length of a competition plus enforced immobility for several hours just after 25 miles (or more) of very active work may tend to make him a little stiff. If he is also fatigued the gentle wander around and the luxurious roll to scratch his hide will do him far more good than a thorough grooming. If the horse is very tired after returning home and it is very late I would do the very minimum about cleaning him. Make him comfortable, but do not fuss. You will probably be tired too. A good grooming the next day in daylight will be quite in order, and if it is hot weather a good wash or sponging is ideal. If the ride day has been very hot you will have sponged him clean after your vetting but prior to bringing him home anyway.

Once the horse has relaxed, if he is in the paddock, put him in his stable. Then feed him his normal rations and allow him all the water he wants. Add a little extra salt to his night feed but not so much that he rejects it. The additional salt will help replace some that is lost through sweat, and normal feeding with access to a saltblock in his paddock will see to the rest over the next couple of days. The normal rations are only for a horse at the lower end of competition. More strenuous rides entail more detailed after-ride care.

Even if a young horse does not find the actual ride that strenuous at the time he is doing it, the competition, plus the drive there and back, and the unusual activities at the venue will combine to tire him more than you would think, and he may not eat all his rations as fast as normal, or he may leave a little. As long as this is only an immediate after-ride reaction and he is eager for his tucker the next morning it is of no account. I do not worry if he does not eat much hay after a ride because he has probably eaten almost a day's ration in the trailer on the journey home. If lack of appetite persists then the ride and the combined extra activities have taken more out of him than they should and it may pay you next time to stay overnight.

When to Stay Overnight

MAXIMUM TRAVEL I have a maximum distance of 100 miles to a venue that I will travel in a day with the ride sandwiched in between. This offers a double safeguard. The horse is not overtaxed and has a chance to relax the night before the ride; more importantly, it ensures that the driver is fresh enough to drive home safely. Some people are not troubled by driving very long distances, but I find that the travelling is by far the hardest part of the event. If you have a co-driver you could stretch it a little further, but remember that travelling does take it out of the horse so limit the distance for his sake as much as the driver's. It is also a good part of the horse's education to stay in a strange stable overnight. If he gets upset by strange surroundings before a 25 miler the effect will not be so bad as the same upset before a really tough Endurance Ride. By the time he has come through the earlier stages of his career staying away from home will not bother him and he will not waste the precious energy that should be conserved for tough rides.

TIMETABLE If you are doing a 25-mile ride, apart from the travel, the table shows the amount of time you can expect to spend.

Amount of time to allow when attending a 25-mile ride

	Maximum	Minimum
Arrival half to one hour before vetting	1 hour	30 mins
Vetting and time to ride start	30 mins	30 mins
Ride done between 6 and 7 m.p.h.	4 hours 10 mins	3 hours 35 mins
Time to post-ride vetting	30 mins	30 mins
Vetting (and possible wait in queue)	15 mins	5 mins
Preparing horse for return journey and loading up	30 mins	30 mins
Time for returning number and collecting award	15 mins	15 mins
Plus there is always the time spent chatting to friends and getting something to eat so a flexible 30 mins or so should be allowed	30 mins	30 mins
TOTAL	7 hours 40 mins	6 hours 25 mins

A little time can be shaved off this if you are very quick at loading up and have a horse clean enough to be comfortable without much brushing, and if you dispense with the socializing after the ride. But in practice I think you will find that competitors do tend to chat a bit after a ride, even if they previously make plans to get away sharply. Of course, if you have a friend with you to share the driving, crew for you on the ride or, using the term that is becoming prevalent in Britain, to act as a gofer (go for this, go for that), much time can be saved.

LONGER RIDE DISTANCES   If you are doing a ride of 40 miles or more you will spend correspondingly more time at the event. Even though the rides will have to be ridden just that little bit faster it will not save much time, as the minimum speed in a higher class is usually the maximum speed required in novice events. I would be even more inclined to stay the night before a very long ride. For the really tough events it is usually one of the rules that horses are stabled the night before, and for the 100 miler the night after as well.

12 Assessing and Conserving the Young Horse

After the Competition

MINI BREAKS   The horse should have a mini holiday after a competition. With a novice horse that you plan to campaign for a whole season it is very important. If the novice horse is also a young animal you should not ask too much in the first season. I think ten or twelve 25 milers are quite sufficient. After each one I give the best part of a week off. The rides will be spaced no closer than two weeks, and usually three or four weeks apart as the season spreads over approximately thirty-five weeks of the year. Obviously if you only intend doing a few 25 milers until you have the confidence to try the longer distances your plan will change, as the 25 milers will then be in the nature of training rides, albeit done at a competition. They will form part of the actual training programme and it will be after the 40 or 50 milers that the horse will have his mini breaks.

ASSESSING THE HORSE'S REACTIONS   After the horse's first competition, or at the latest after his second attempt, you should be able to assess whether he is fit enough for the 25-mile distance you are asking. The way he reacts after the ride should inform you of his real condition. Does he bounce back as if nothing has happened? Do his legs fill after staying in the stable the night after the competition? Is he free moving or a bit stiff the morning after when he is turned out? Is his appetite good? Is his general behaviour full of sparkle? A lot of questions, but if the answers point to vitality and eagerness for more he is fit and the competition has done him good.

Early Penalties

Do not be alarmed if there are one or two areas where the horse acquires penalties. Young and/or inexperienced horses frequently have an elevated heart rate at rides. This is not necessarily because of bad preparation but just sheer excitement, and an elevated heart rate is not always indicative of lack of fitness. By the time you have done enough training, and also kept your particular long distance horse a considerable time, you should be able to differentiate between an elevated heart rate due to excitement and one due to fatigue. The way the horse moves under you will be a very good guide. Frequently the young horse will be calm on the trail, only becoming unsettled when he returns to the venue. This effect will gradually diminish as the season progresses and as the horse gets more accustomed to going to different places. The present system of a scale of penalties for certain heart-rate figures does not allow the veterinary surgeons to make any judgement in the matter, and I have had several veterinary surgeons acknowledge that with an excitable horse, the heart rate does not always reflect his true condition, so be assured on this point. If there is cause for alarm you will definitely be warned by the veterinary surgeon who monitors the horse throughout the competition. Long distance riding horses who compete regularly have the added bonus of repeated veterinary checks throughout the season, so any incipient trouble will be bound to show up and the owner/rider be alerted before real trouble or damage is caused.

The young and inexperienced horse may acquire penalties if he brushes. Minor scuff marks on the hooves are no longer penalized. Young horses that do not yet have their full adult muscling in the inner thigh area often travel closer behind than they will in another season or so, when maturity coupled with conditioning will have increased muscle bulk, giving them a wider track behind. If the young horse knocks himself occasionally much can be done to alleviate this problem by clever shoeing. Setting the shoes slightly under the hoof so the inner edge of the shoe does not strike the opposite fetlock helps. If the horse still brushes it will be the lesser blow of horn, not metal, that connects. This problem can also be alleviated on a running repair basis by bevelling the inner edge of the shoe with the rasp carried as part of your kit. A rounded edge is less hazardous than a flat, sharp edge. If the damage is severe it probably stems from bad conformation. Tiredness also makes the horse prone to self-inflicted damage. A badly schooled horse is more likely to damage himself than one who is trained and ridden efficiently. Some horses only brush if they are pushed on too hard into a gait that is not natural for them, so it behoves the rider to try to correct his own riding methods if this is the case. One other possible cause is just sheer laziness. Some horses are idle and do not use themselves efficiently, but they are often partnered by a rider who could do with a bit of waking up as well.

It is not always the horse with the perfect veterinary score that is the better animal. Many young horses that have a super season in low distances never grade up, or if they do, do not capitalize on that initial promise. Other youngsters take a season to learn the ropes and come into their own. It takes time for them to learn to use themselves efficiently, cope with all sorts of going, and become inured to venue activity. Many horses get good gradings in low distanced rides, but later at 40 and 50 miles they will struggle to achieve high marks, while the horse that has had a slow start and not been over-used may well get better and better. Many top endurance horses had only moderate results in C.T.R. but when really challenged showed their true mettle.

Maintenance

Once the horse is fit it is not necessary to ride him as often as in early training. With a novice or young horse limited to short distances, after he has had his five days to a week off, I will ride him every other day and cover between 6 and 10 miles. Provided the next ride is no more than three weeks away from the previous one I find that one additional long ride of 15 to 18 miles is quite sufficient, done in the middle of the week prior to his next event. If it is a month away I will slip two long training rides in during the three weeks of interim work. If there is only a two-week gap between rides I will not do more than the 6 to 10 miles' distance. The actual competition will be his long ride and substitute for the long training day. One exception to this is when working with a horse whose head needs sorting out more than its body. For the flighty horse that only settles with very regular work I would at least do a moderate hacking type of ride on most days of the week just to keep the horse civil.

UNDEREXERCISING Do not take the opposite attitude that it is sufficient just to do the competitions. I know some riders get away with it, but I do not think they would continue to do so once the distances creep up, and more pressure is put on the horse. They are cheating the horse. Repeatedly doing long competitive rides without sufficient maintenance work will eventually put an accumulated strain on the horse that may not show until the damage is done, and he either goes lame, gets into the very poor, run up, excessively lean state that indicates undue stress over a long period, or starts to get bad grades for no apparent reason, whereas before he succeeded with good scores.

It is all too easy to slip into the habit of delaying riding the horse because he is, or you think he is, fit from the previous event. It will be a habit hard to break and very dangerous when you start your second season at longer distances. A long distance horse's training should not only be on a yearly basis, but if you intend to become fully involved should be a progressively worked out scheme planned over a two- to three-year period until he has peaked at major ride ability.

13 Budgeting

At the beginning of the season work out your budget. Make a list with several headings or sections. It should contain what you would like to do with your horse as far as competitions go; the expenses that you will incur in order to make it possible to enter competitions; the additional expenses envisaged on top of the maintenance costs you already have in keeping a horse; travel costs; once only expenses.

Annual Expenses

These are incurred in order to be able to participate. They include:

Membership fees to the society(ies) whose rules you intend riding under.

Annual booster for vaccinations against equine influenza.

Annual subscription to the Automobile Association which should include Relay Supplement that will cover bringing the horse and your trailer home. It is worth the peace of mind to have it.

Entry fees. You can work out in advance from the fixture lists how much these will cost per annum.

TRAVEL TO VENUES Plan your season by choosing the rides you think would be most suitable. For a newcomer this usually means selecting the rides that entail the least amount of travelling to venues. Some riders are lucky and live centrally to quite a number of rides and can plan a season where they will never have to drive over 75 miles to a venue. Others who live on the fringe of the busy long distance riding groups will probably have quite a few rides within reasonable distance, but will occasionally need to travel further afield if they plan to compete on a fairly regular basis.

At present I live in a very bad area for long distance riding, right in the heart of the Cambridgeshire Fens. The land is flat and very uninteresting and lacks a real challenge, other than that of getting out and doing monotonous miles of training in unvarying countryside. Up to a couple of years ago the closest ride was 75 miles away, but even in such an outpost things are changing. For those who find their first season's choice throws up a succession of flat rides it is important that in the ensuing season they make the effort to choose rides of a more challenging nature, even if it means further travelling. Cost of travelling tends to be the biggest deciding factor as to where you choose to compete, but to round out a horse's conditioning programme once he is away from novice stage do make the effort to try the more difficult rides, even if you have to curtail the number you do in order to be more selective.

For a ten-ride introductory season with a young horse I travelled an average of 200 miles per ride, the closest being 50 miles distant, the furthest nearly 150 miles away. I stayed overnight twice, and should have done so three times but had miscalculated badly on the distance for one ride. Rides ranged from Yorkshire to Leicester on a north to south basis, and into the Midlands as far as Worcestershire. With the exception of those who live in Scotland and who want to do a series of rides further south I think that this works out at a very reasonable average that could be a good guide for most riders entering the sport. Wales is particularly well catered for. Nearly all major rides, with the exception of one or two of the major B.H.S. L.D.R.G. events, have multiple classes catering for the very experienced, the up and coming, and the completely novice horse and/or rider. The cost of travel for a ten-ride season, which is ample for a newcomer, can therefore be worked out on the basis of 2,000 miles of driving. Each person will know what their own vehicle does to the gallon. There will be extra wear on tyres necessitating more frequent purchase, and the more regular servicing of your vehicle(s). They all need to be budgeted for.

OVERNIGHT ACCOMMODATION   There will be two or three overnight stops where cost of stabling for the horse and accommodation for the rider must be considered. Both are usually moderately priced, unless you opt for the added expense of better accommodation for the rider. Many riders camp out or sleep in the horsebox, being satisfied if the horse is comfortable. I do not recommend it, as I dislike having to 'rough it'. I have done my share of that, but others actually enjoy that aspect. The choice is yours! Eating out also has to be added to the cost of the occasional overnight stops, and most riders make for the nearest pub where good food is generally easy to come by. It is also a good gathering place for other overnight endurance riders and makes the evening enjoyable.

By the time you have graduated from novice rides to the longer rides where it will be necessary to stay overnight more often you will know if you want to undertake the added expense. By that time too you will probably want to look for a greater variety in the terrain rides are run over, particularly if in your first season you stuck close to home. A great number of rides are run over undemanding country, as I found in the above-mentioned novice season. That did surprise me considering the spread of the rides. Some people are lucky in having demanding going as their home locale.

Weekly and Monthly Bills

The other areas of expense are in the higher costs of actually maintaining a horse for distance work.

FEED COSTS A novice horse will need an increase in his hard feed rations, and consequently the feed bill will rise, but not very dramatically, unless you have been relying on grazing for summer feed. In that case you will notice a considerable increase, as he must have sufficient hard food to enable him to maintain condition and fuel his energy bank for competition. If he is also a relatively young horse he will not be fully mature and will need more food than an older horse. When my stallion Nizzolan did his first Golden Horseshoe Rides at ages five and six, he ate 17 lb of hard feed a day. As an eight-year-old horse when he won the first British 100 miler he only ate 15 lb. That was for a tougher ride yet he consumed fewer concentrates.

SUPPLEMENTS   I do not think a horse in moderate, novice level competition should need supplements if his diet consists of top quality feeds. However, if it is difficult to obtain first quality, some supplement may be required. Be advised by your veterinary surgeon, not the glossy advertisements, as to which you should use. If your horse's hooves are shelly or have poor growth he may need a specially formulated supplement. I use Biotin on my farrier's recommendation. In exceptionally hot weather electrolytes are most necessary, especially for very stressful rides. They should not be essential for a 25-mile novice horse that is not being ridden at maximum output.

SHOEING   Several extra visits by the farrier will need to be budgeted for.

Once in a While Purchases

If you have never competed in any sort of event before there will be the once only (or at most only very occasional) purchases such as travelling rugs, coolers, leg wraps, stethoscope, water containers, and various pieces of spare equipment, especially girths, reins, stirrup leathers and saddle pads. It sounds a lot, but most horse owners do acquire more than the minimum amount of equipment and items can be added to gradually.

The foregoing paragraphs on budgeting may seem alarming but it is much better to understand what you are letting yourself in for than to rush into the sport totally unprepared and find you can only accomplish half the rides you had hoped to. It is a sport that does not have expensive frills, but nevertheless there are unavoidable costs, and the more you are involved naturally the higher they go, but having said that they are not nearly as high as keeping a showjumper or a showhorse, where the costs are the same whether the horse wins, places, or comes nowhere. All horses who successfully complete a long distance ride course earn an award. The sport is a compulsive one, or in my experience has been so for myself and for hundreds of riders I know, who really do not know why they get up at unsocial hours, travel in inclement weather, spend hard-earned cash on driving 100 miles to an event to ride 25 miles, and come home tired out but *elated*. But the riders do it repeatedly; the horses love it; and it does become a way of life where the costs are borne without a grumble. Many long distance riders have that as their only hobby, so other aspects such as holidays are subjugated in favour of the long distance trail and the tremendous companionship of a fit, healthy, competitive horse.

4 Tack

When choosing tack for the long distance horse the prime requirements are fit and comfort for both horse and rider. There are no rule restrictions regarding the type of saddle used, and bridles may be of any type provided bitting is of a humane variety. Draw reins, side reins and check reins are prohibited.

Any lesions or bruising caused by ill-fitting equipment will be penalized. If these should be severe enough the horse may be withdrawn by the presiding veterinary surgeon(s), or eliminated at the finish of a ride if the damage is considered too severe to permit the horse to proceed further.

Saddles

Saddles fall into three broad categories: the spring-tree English saddle; the rigid-tree English saddle; and the Western saddle.

THE FITTING OF A SADDLE   Apart from the desirable good fit a major consideration when choosing a saddle is how much of the horse's back the bars of the tree cover. Within reason the bigger the bars the more the load is spread over the back. One of the main areas of concern is where a horse gets pressure bumps caused by too much pressure being located in too small an area. These can be caused by a saddle that is even slightly unsuited to the horse's back. In normal two- or three-hour sessions there will be no problems, but when the horse has to bear weight and is very active over an extended period of time any discrepancy in fit will become increasingly more of an aggravation. If the problem is really bad it will show up even in a 25 miler, but most saddle problems do not make themselves evident until the horse has

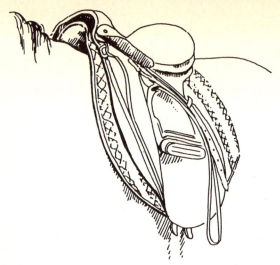

Correctly fitting English saddle. Note the saddle pad pulled up into the gullet to prevent pressure and allow an air channel.

upgraded to the 40 mile plus category and is being ridden for many hours at a stretch. The tell-tale signs of a horse that has had old saddle pressure bumps are the white patches of hair just behind the withers and about two to three inches below the spine. If the pressure has been excessive not only will a bump appear but the hair follicles will be damaged, causing the hair to come out, along with a thickened patch of skin which gradually sloughs off through the new hair that grows. It is this new hair that frequently comes through white.

The problem can often be cured by attention to the saddle stuffing. Sometimes pressure bumps are caused by the rider distributing his/her weight unevenly over the horse's back. This is not as uncommon as would first appear because if a rider has any personal 'conformation' fault it may make him/her ride more to one side than the other. Some riders place more pressure on one stirrup than the other which is reflected in weight distribution. Many people suffer from intermittent lower back pain, riders amongst them, and especially towards the latter stages of a very long ride this may cause discomfort which may be reflected in the way the rider sits. I myself had been raising a welt on horses, always in exactly the same place no matter what saddle I used, or how much care was taken to ensure good fit, and never until I had ridden 40 miles or more. I had not linked an old back injury and the pressure bumps until an X-ray revealed that my spine is slightly crooked. Since then I have taken more than usual notice of other riders, and many very good riders do not sit in the saddle with 100 per cent even weight distribution.

WESTERN SADDLES A Western saddle nearly always offers a better weight distribution because of its basic structure. If one is chosen make sure it is used in conjunction with a very thick pad or folded blanket, as the conch roundels for securing the leather thongs that are used to tie equipment on are sometimes secured right through the tree, especially on a cheaper saddle. There is no stuffing to worry about with a Western saddle, but the pad used with it must be of good quality, absorbent and non-slip.

The saddle should fit the horse well, so be careful to choose the correct gullet width. It should also fit the horse supremely well in the cantle area, as otherwise the rear housing of the leather can sometimes rub quite badly while the horse is working for many hours. Western saddles are secured by a variety of different knots or buckles. The knotted variety nearly always causes discomfort for the rider because the knot comes just under the knee area.

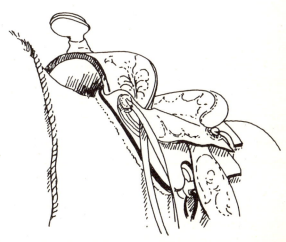

Correctly fitting Western saddle, with good gullet clearance. This saddle is shown without a pad to demonstrate fitting, but a Western saddle should *never* be used without a thick pad or folded blanket.

95

Over a long ride this could become more and more of a hindrance. Most quality saddles have one of the many good buckle devices for securing girths.

The better quality Western saddles are usually considerably heavier than the cheaper variety, and provided the weight is not too great it should not cause concern. Nowadays there are more top quality lightweight Western saddles being produced, some indeed specifically for distance riding, and there are several suppliers in Great Britain who advertise in the 'horsy press' so purchase is easier than it used to be. Western saddles tend to keep their place on the horse's back better, not being inclined to rock in the gullet when climbing up hills, as do some of their English counterparts. A good Western saddle is comfortable, but a poor quality one is murder to ride in. Weights range from super lightweights on a par with English saddle weights, to the really heavy 40 lb plus, to which is added the 4 or 5 lb of pad, but a serviceable saddle of a good quality should be available at 20 to 25 lb or so. Contrary to many people's thinking a few extra pounds in weight is not going to affect the horse's performance. A badly fitting saddle most definitely will.

ENGLISH SADDLES If using an English saddle the rigid tree is preferable to the spring tree. The latter is subject to metal stress, and the actual tree is not so large as that of a rigid variety. The rigid-tree saddle offers a greater load-bearing surface. English saddles also come in several gullet widths, so be careful to use one appropriate to your own horse's conformation. If the gullet is too narrow it will pinch the wither area and also give a bad fit to the top of the shoulder. If it is too wide the saddle will drop on to the withers, and with the rider's weight in the saddle cause untold back problems. A good guide is to see if you can easily see through the saddle from front arch to the cantle with a clear channel right through, and when mounted easily pass a flexible crop through from front to rear. The English saddle that fits the horse at the beginning of training may need adjustment in padding by the time the horse is really fit, as the wither area and the back will fine down as the horse's fitness improves. If you do have to have the saddle restuffed ensure the old stuffing is removed, teased out, and replaced with additional material. If additional material is just rammed in without taking the old out pressure points could be created, with resultant problems. When taking your saddle in for this type of treatment make a point of requesting this be done. Many years ago I was caught out by a so-called saddler and paid the penalty, until I found a really good craftsman to rectify the job. It is not sufficient merely to add extra saddle pads to overcome discrepancy in saddle fit.

NUMNAHS   Any numnahs used with English saddles should be absorbent and thick enough to afford a little cushioning, but not so thick that they force the bars of the tree apart. Also, too thick a pad will cause the saddle to roll when the horse is in motion. The type of pad with the foam interleaved between cotton or mock sheepskin is not suitable. The saddle tends to shift around with the constant squeezing effect of the foam. When siting the pad on the horse's back make sure it is properly fitted so it cannot slip when the horse is in motion. It should not pull down and exert pressure over the withers, as this can cause soreness.

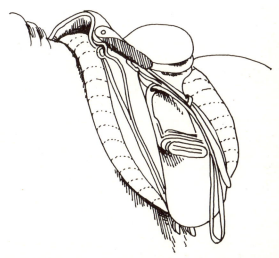

Incorrect fitting of numnah, putting pressure on the withers which will cause soreness. This type of pad is too thick and may cause the saddle to move.

Bridles and other tack

BRIDLES   Bridles should fit well, not being too tight, especially in the noseband or throatlatch area as this would restrict breathing. Nor should they slop about too loosely. Bitting should be smooth, properly adjusted, and if a curb strap or chain is fitted care should be taken over securing it so that it does not pinch or rub. One of the examinations always made by the veterinary surgeon is to see if the horse has any mouth lacerations or bruising.

BREASTPLATES   At some stage in a horse's career a breastplate will be necessary, even if the horse does not normally wear one. They are very useful for hill work as they prevent a saddle slipping on a steep incline. The type best suited for distance riding is the hunting breastplate that attaches to the rings on either side of the saddle pommel. The straps that come down the shoulders should preferably be of rounded leather so there are no cutting edges to exert pressure when the horse is going up or down a steep hill. This type does not in any way restrict his air intake. The type that goes straight across the chest and is secured to the girth can press into the windpipe when upward or downward thrust is exerted. If you cannot buy (or have made) the rounded leather type purchase a wide strapped variety. Western breastcollars also come in two types – one straight across the chest similar to the one described above but of wider leather, and the contoured V-shaped type. Choose the V-shaped one in sufficient width to spread pressure. Have it fleece-lined for comfort and sweat absorption.

I have only dealt with aspects of tack that specifically influence the wellbeing of the distance horse, all other equipment being left to the discretion of the rider who will know the best type of a certain item to choose.

False Economy

It is not an economy to purchase the cheapest equipment. Distance horses wear tack for many hours at a stretch, and for more days in the week than the average saddle horse. Equipment will

Good type of breastplate for a Western saddle, which will not interfere with the breathing.

be subjected to much hard usage so get the best you can afford, and in the matter of a saddle either have the saddler come out and fit the horse or take the horse to the saddler. Keep everything in a supple condition, paying attention to oiling, as there will undoubtedly be many occasions when tack gets thoroughly soaked during a season, consequently drying stiff and uncomfortable.

15 Assistance on a Ride

I have always found it a luxury to have someone crewing for me and over the years have learned to cope adequately without an assistant. However, I do make arrangements for help at the more strenuous rides.

At some longer B.H.S. rides it is mandatory to have an assistant available to help with the care of the horse at veterinary checkpoints and at ride starts and finishes. At other rides, because of the route length and because mandatory stops will be out on course, it is advisable to have such help.

Most newcomers to the sport will be entering the shorter distanced rides at first with distances ranging from 20 to 30 miles. These rides do not have a mandatory halt, the whole distance being ridden in one section. There may be the occasional spot check by a veterinary surgeon. If you have an assistant for these rides it is a definite bonus, but even for a newcomer who is unfamiliar with the sport it is quite possible to manage on your own.

Managing Solo

The keyword to this is organization, and also a well-mannered horse. If you have organized everything you will need in the correct sequence and ready to hand in your vehicle, much time and frustration will be saved. The horse should have been well trained so you can work over him efficiently. If he is constantly yanking at his lead rope to get at grass, which will be followed by wandering off in pursuit of more, you have a problem. I expect my own horses to stand calmly with their heads up while I attend to them. It takes perseverance and discipline to achieve but it is worth it. If you can tie him in absolute safety do so, but the average ride venue, particularly the area where the boxes and trailers are parked, is very crowded and people, horses and dogs are constantly moving around. It seems as if half the canine population are constant participants at rides, and they are frequently not under control, even though ride regulations stipulate in some of their literature that such control is necessary. I remember a veterinary surgeon once commenting at a ride with a very large equine entry that there were more dogs than horses around. For this reason alone it is better to have a longer lead rope than normal and maintain contact with your horse while you are attending to him. A normal length one is not sufficient when you are cleaning his hindquarters, or picking out his hind feet.

If you do not have your own 'crewperson' there is always someone who is willing to give occasional help. Frequently you do not even have to ask but a complete stranger will come up and offer to hold your horse, or help with unloading; but do not be frightened to ask. Such help is *never* refused. This is one of the attractions of the sport and one not so readily found in the show scene.

PLANNING   End of ride care is made a lot easier if, when you arrived earlier and before you even went to the veterinary surgeon for pre-ride vetting, you made sure your water, bucket(s), cooler, and cleaning gear were all ready to be used on your return. If you do have someone crewing for you make sure you have discussed in detail what will be necessary and in what order, so he/she is efficient when you return to ride base.

Having a Crew

RESPONSIBILITY   The onus for the horse's care is on you, not your assistant, though in the case of an emergency the assistant should be able to take over and do everything for the horse, including taking it to the veterinary surgeon for its post-ride examination. Your assistant should practise at home so that he/she is familiar with handling your horse and the horse is also relaxed with the assistant. It can make quite a difference at the final vetting if the horse should be uneasy with a total stranger.

Quite a high percentage of helpers at rides do not have much to do with handling horses, but are drafted in to help.

ON-COURSE STOPS On longer rides where there are mandatory stops which are often away from the main ride base, it is very important that whoever is crewing for you knows exactly what you will need and when to expect you. Well before the ride study the map so that whoever is driving knows how to get to the mid-ride checkpoint. Work out an approximate time schedule with a minimum, probable, and maximum expected time of arrival. If the ride is one you have had to travel to the night before it is well worth that little bit of extra driving to find out exactly where this checkpoint is and do a trial run the night before. With the one mandatory stop usual on a ride demanding moderate speeds it will be sufficient to be met *only* at the half-way point.

HIGH PERFORMANCE RIDES When you have gained the experience to attempt the longer rides that demand both higher speeds and the longer distances, such as the B.H.S. Gold Series, E.H.P.S. Endurance Rides, and H.L.D.R.C. Endurance and Championship rides, an assistant is absolutely necessary, particularly out on course. The timetable of E.T.A.s will have to be very carefully worked out, as will all the places you want to be met en route. In some cases it will prove quite difficult for the helper to get there before the rider. Going via country lanes the driver may have to do considerably more mileage than the rider, where a ridden section is only a short distance between spots accessible to a vehicle at road crossings. The main requirements en route, particularly on a very hot day, will be water for the horse with electrolytes added if necessary, a drink for the rider, and a wipe over with a sponge for the horse's face – it refreshes him if he is hot and sticky. At the main checkpoints, where there is a timed holdover and a veterinary examination, equipment will have to be attended to – clean saddle pads; clean girth; a quick look at the horse's shoes to see all is in order; at major rides there is a farrier who will go out on course calls to horses with lost or loose shoes. The horse will have to be attended to rapidly and without fuss. If it is a hot day a sponge-over with cool but not icy water will refresh him; water with the chill off in moderate amounts should be offered to him to drink. If it is a cold day clean him rapidly, but get a blanket over his back as a chill wind can make him stiffen, particularly in the loin and hind leg area. If he has come in very fast do not let him stand about for the whole time, particularly if it is an hour's holdover. Just before he is due to be presented to the veterinary surgeon for a run up he should be very gently walked. His heart rate needs to stay down, but his limbs also need to be functioning well.

A thorough trial run of all you expect your assistant to do at a ride should have been done at home. The tougher the ride the more you will rely on a good crew attending to the horse at holdovers. *But you have the ultimate responsibility.* Whoever is helping you must be prepared to do it your way, unless it is obvious that he/she is already very well experienced from the actual competing side of endurance riding. If you have a temporarily grounded top endurance rider for a crew you are very lucky! Only the rider knows how the horse feels under him, what energy has been expended in previous sections, and what the horse's mental state is. Be prepared to alter prior plans at a moments notice, and make sure your assistant can also respond to a sudden change. If you do have that gem of a helper, the experienced endurance rider, you can learn a lot about after-ride care by noting how he or she cares for a horse at holdovers after a tough ride. An experienced crewperson can make the difference between a horse passing or not passing the vet in a very tough ride.

Conclusion

From my own experience of many types of competitive riding I can say that there is no branch of equestrian sport that offers such a sense of sheer achievement as that of long distance riding. Along with the achievement goes the attractive bonus of riding in some of the most beautiful parts of the British Isles – parts still unspoilt, and on many of the really long tough rides routes laid over little known territory: the scarps of Welsh mountains; the purple haze of New Forest heathland; the clear rills of Dartmoor streams; the rocky boulder-strewn tracks of historic Exmoor; the sweeps of the South Downs; and many more enchanting areas. Added to this are the friendships made and the sense of co-operation, rather than knife-edge competition.

If this book helps the newcomer to the sport to achieve some of the pleasure I have had from long distance riding by easing his or her path through the first few rides I shall be well satisfied. Even more to the point, if it helps riders prepare and compete with their horses so that they too enjoy the activity, it will have served its purpose.